TestSMART®

for Reading Skills and Comprehension—Grade 5

Help for
Basic Reading Skills
State Competency Tests
Achievement Tests

by

Lori Mammen

These popular series of books are available from ECS Learning Systems, Inc.

Structures for Reading, Writing, Thinking	Gr. 4-9	4 Titles
Writing Warm-Ups™	Gr. K–6 & 7–12	4 Titles
Foundations for Writing	Gr. 2–8	2 Titles
Springboards for Reading	Gr. 3–6 & 7–12	2 Titles
Booklinks to American and World History	Gr. 4–8	12 Titles
The Picture Book Companion	Gr. K–3	3 Titles
Novel Extenders	Gr. 1–6	7 Titles
Literature Guides	Gr. 7–12	17 Titles
Building Language Power	Gr. 4–9	3 Titles
Quick Thinking™	Gr. K–12	2 Titles
Thematic Units	Gr. K–8	23 Titles
Activity Books	Gr. K–12	11 Titles
EnviroLearn™	Gr. K–5	5 Titles
Home Study Collection™(Basic Skills & More)	Gr. 1–6	18 Titles
Test Preparation Guides	Gr. 2–12	41 Titles

Other Activity Books		
Not More Writing?!	Gr. 9–12	
Passageways Gr. 5-9		
Booklinks	Gr. 3–8	
Tactics to Tackle Thinking	Gr. 6–12	

Brown Bag Science	Gr. 1–4	16 Titles
Wake Up, Brain!!	Gr. 1–6	6 Titles

To order, contact your local school supply store, or write/call for a complete catalog:

ECS Learning Systems, Inc.
P.O. Box 440
Bulverde, Texas 78163-0440

www.educyberstor.com

Editor: Jennifer L. Sullivan **Cover:** Kirstin Simpson **Book Design:** Educational Media Services

ISBN 1–57022–200–2

Contents

Welcome to *TestSMART* ®!!

It's just the tool you need
to help students review important reading skills and
prepare for standardized reading tests!

Introduction

During the past several years, an increasing number of American students have faced some form of state-mandated competency testing in reading. While several states use established achievement tests, such as the Iowa Test of Basic Skills (ITBS), to assess students' reading ability, other states' reading assessments focus on the skills and knowledge emphasized in their particular reading curriculum. Texas, for example, has administered the state-developed assessment since 1990. The New York State Testing Program began in 1999 and tests both fourth- and eighth-grade students in reading.

Whatever the testing route, one point is very clear: the trend toward more and more competency testing is widespread and intense. By the spring of 1999, 48 states had adopted some type of reading assessment for students at various grade levels. In some states, these tests are "high-stakes" events that determine whether a student is promoted to the next grade level in school.

The emphasis on competency tests has grown directly from the national push for higher educational standards and accountability. Under increasing pressure from political leaders, business people, and the general public, policy-makers have turned to testing as a primary way to measure and improve student performance. Although experienced educators know that such test results can reveal only a small part of a much broader educational picture, state-mandated competency tests have gained a strong foothold. Teachers must find effective ways to help their students prepare for these tests—and this is where *TestSMART* ® plays an important role.

What's inside this book?

Designed to help students review and practice important reading and test-taking skills, *TestSMART* ® includes reproducible practice exercises in the following areas—

* vocabulary
* comprehension
* study skills

In addition, each *TestSMART* ® book includes—

* a master skills list based on reading standards of several states
* a comprehensive vocabulary list
* complete answer keys for multiple-choice questions
* scoring guidelines and rubrics for open-ended questions
* a reproducible answer sheet

4

The content of each section of *TestSMART®* is outlined below.

Vocabulary: This section of *TestSMART®* includes 18 practice exercises with questions that focus on—

- demonstrating knowledge of synonyms (Practices 1–3)
- demonstrating knowledge of antonyms (Practices 4–6)
- demonstrating knowledge of homonyms (Practice 7–9)
- using context clues to determine word meaning (Practices 10–12)
- recognizing the correct meaning of a word with multiple meanings (Practices 13–15)
- demonstrating knowledge of word analogies (Practices 16–18)

(Note: Vocabulary skills addressed in this section are also addressed in the reading comprehension section of TestSMART® *.)*

Comprehension: This section of *TestSMART®* includes—

- 15 reading passages, which include nonfiction, fiction, and poetry selections
- multiple-choice and open-ended questions for each passage
- tag-lines that identify the skill(s) addressed in each question

Reading skills addressed in this section include—

- determining the meaning of words *(root words, context clues, multiple-meaning words, synonyms/antonyms)*

- identifying supporting ideas *(facts/details, sequential order, written directions, setting)*
- summarizing written texts *(main idea, summary of major ideas/themes/ procedures)*
- perceiving relationships and recognizing outcomes *(cause/effect, predictions, similarities/differences)*
- analyzing information to make inferences and generalizations *(inferences, interpretations/ conclusions, generalizations, character analysis)*
- recognizing points of view, propaganda, and statements of fact/opinion *(fact/opinion, author's purpose)*
- reading, analyzing, and interpreting literature *(genre identification, genre characteristics, literary elements, figurative language)*

Study Skills: This section of *TestSMART®* includes 11 practice exercises that focus on identifying and using sources of different types of information (graphic sources, parts of a book, dictionary skills). Specific skills addressed in this section include—

- using an index in a book (Practice 1)
- using the table of contents in a book (Practice 2)
- identifying appropriate sources of information (Practice 3)
- recognizing and using dictionary skills (Practices 4, 9–10)
- using a library card catalog (Practices 5–6)
- interpreting graphs (Practices 7–8)
- interpreting a map (Practice 11)

Master Skills List/Correlation Chart: The reading skills addressed in *TestSMART*® are based on the reading standards and/or test specifications from several different states. No two states have identical wordings for their skills lists, but there are strong similarities from one state's list to another. Of course, the skills needed for effective reading do not change from one place to another. The Master Skills List for Reading (page 9) represents a synthesis of the reading skills emphasized in various states. Teachers who use this book will recognize the skills that are stressed, even though the wording of a few objectives may vary slightly from that found in their own state's test specifications. The Master Skills Correlation Chart (page 10) offers a place to identify the skills common to both *TestSMART*® and a specific state competency test.

Vocabulary List: A list of vocabulary words appears on page 127. This list includes many of the words tested in the vocabulary section of this book and in questions that accompany some of the passages. Teachers and students can use this list to create—

- word games
- word walls
- writing activities
- "word-of-the-day" activities
- synonym/antonym charts
- word webs
- analogies
- …and more

A word of caution: In general, teachers should not ask students to memorize the words and their meanings. While some tests ask students to simply "know" the meaning of selected vocabulary words,

the majority of tests emphasize using structural cues and context clues to determine the meaning of unfamiliar words encountered during reading.

Answer Keys: Complete answer keys for multiple-choice questions appear on pages 119–121.

Scoring Guidelines and Rubrics: The scoring guidelines and sample rubrics on pages 122–126 provide important information for evaluating responses to open-ended questions. *(Note: If a state's assessment does not include open-ended questions, teachers may use the open-ended items in* TestSMART® *as appropriate for their students.)* The scoring guidelines indicate the expected contents of successful responses. For example, if an open-ended question asks students to create a new title for a passage and give reasons for their answer, the scoring guideline for that question suggests specific points that students should include in the answer.

The sample rubrics allow teachers to rate the overall effectiveness and thoroughness of an answer. Once again, consider the example of creating a new title for a passage and supporting the answer with specific reasons. The corresponding rubric for that question indicates the number and quality of the reasons necessary to earn a score of "4" (for an effective, complete response) or a score of "1" (for an ineffective, incomplete response).

How to Use This Book

Effective Test Preparation: What is the most effective way to prepare students for any reading competency test? Experienced educators know that the best test preparation includes three critical components—

- a strong curriculum that includes the content and skills to be tested
- effective and varied instructional methods that allow students to learn content and skills in many different ways
- targeted practice that familiarizes students with the specific content and format of the test they will take

Obviously, a strong curriculum and effective, varied instructional methods provide the foundation for all appropriate test preparation. Contrary to what some might believe, merely "teaching the test" performs a great disservice to students. Students must acquire knowledge, practice skills, and have specific educational experiences which can never be included on tests limited by time and in scope. For this reason, books like *TestSMART* ® should **never** become the heart of the curriculum or a replacement for strong instructional methods.

Targeted Practice: *TestSMART* ® does, however, address the final element of effective test preparation (targeted test practice) in the following ways—

- *TestSMART* ® familiarizes students with the content usually included in competency tests.
- *TestSMART* ® familiarizes students with the general format of such tests.

When students become familiar with both the content and the format of a test, they know what to expect on the actual test. This, in turn, improves their chances for success.

Using *TestSMART* ®: Used as part of the regular curriculum, *TestSMART* ® allows teachers to—

- pretest skills needed for the actual test students will take
- determine students' areas of strength and/or weakness
- provide meaningful test-taking practice for students
- ease students' test anxiety
- communicate test expectations and content to parents

Other Suggestions for Instruction: *TestSMART* ® can serve as a springboard for other effective instructional activities that help with test preparation.

Group Work: Teacher and students work through selected practice exercises together, noting the kinds of questions and the range of answer choices. They discuss common errors for each kind of question and strategies for avoiding these errors.

Predicting Answers: Students predict the correct answer before reading the given answer choices. This encourages students to think through the question rather than focus on finding the right answer. Students then read the given answer choices and determine which one, if any, matches the answer they have given.

7

Developing Test Questions: Once students become familiar with the format of test questions, they develop "test-type" questions for other assigned   reading (e.g., science, social studies).

Vocabulary Development: Teachers and students foster vocabulary development in all subject areas through the use of word walls, word webs, word games, synonym/antonym charts, analogies, word categories, "word-of-the-day" activities, etc.

Two-Sentence Recaps: Students regularly summarize what they have read in one or two sentences. For fiction, students use the basic elements (setting, characters, problem, solution) to guide their summaries. For nonfiction, students use the journalist's questions (who, what, where, when, why) for the same purpose. The teacher may also list 3–5 key words from a reading selection and direct students to write a one- to two-sentence summary that includes the given words.

Generalizations: After students read a selection, the teacher states a generalization based on the reading, and students provide specific facts and details to support the generalization; or the teacher provides specifics from the selection, and students state the generalization.

Master Skills List

I. Determine the meaning of words in written texts
   A. Use root words and other structural cues to recognize new words
   B. Use context clues to determine word meaning
   C. Recognize correct meaning of words with multiple meanings
   D. Demonstrate knowledge of synonyms, antonyms, and homophones

II. Identify supporting ideas
   A. Identify relevant facts and details
   B. Sequence events in chronological order (e.g., story events, steps in process)
   C. Follow written directions
   D. Identify the importance of setting to a story's meaning

III. Summarize a variety of written texts
   A. Determine the main idea or essential message of a text
   B. Summarize the major ideas, themes, or procedures of a text

IV. Perceive relationships and recognize outcomes
   A. Identify cause and effect relationships in a text
   B. Make and verify predictions with information from text
   C. Identify similarities and differences in text(s) (e.g., topics, characters)

V. Analyze information in order to make inferences and generalizations
   A. Make and explain inferences (e.g., main idea, conclusion, moral, cause/effect)
   B. Support interpretations/conclusions with information from a text
   C. Make generalizations based on information from a text
   D. Analyze characters (e.g., traits, feelings, relationships) from a story

VI. Recognize points of view, propaganda, and statements of fact and opinion
   A. Distinguish fact from opinion in a text
   B. Identify the author's purpose

VII. Read, analyze, and interpret literature
   A. Identify genres of fiction, nonfiction, and poetry
   B. Identify characteristics representative of a given genre
   C. Identify important literary elements (e.g., theme, plot, character) in a text
   D. Recognize/interpret figurative language (e.g., simile, metaphor)

VIII. Identify and use sources of different types of information
   A. Use and interpret graphic sources of information (e.g., charts, graphs)
   B. Use reference resources and the parts of a book (e.g., index) to locate information
   C. Recognize and use dictionary skills

Master Skills Correlation Chart

Use this chart to identify the *TestSMART*® skills included on a specific state competency test. Place a check mark next to those skills common to both.

I.	**Determine the meaning of words in written texts**	
	A. Use root words and other structural cues to recognize new words	
	B. Use context clues to determine word meaning	
	C. Recognize correct meaning of words with multiple meanings	
	D. Demonstrate knowledge of synonyms, antonyms, and homophones	
II.	**Identify supporting ideas**	
	A. Identify relevant facts and details	
	B. Sequence events in chronological order	
	C. Follow written directions	
	D. Identify the importance of setting to a story's meaning	
III.	**Summarize a variety of written texts**	
	A. Determine the main idea or essential message of a text	
	B. Summarize the major ideas, themes, or procedures of a text	
IV.	**Perceive relationships and recognize outcomes**	
	A. Identify cause and effect relationships in a text	
	B. Make and verify predictions with information from text	
	C. Identify similarities and differences in text(s)	
V.	**Analyze information in order to make inferences and generalizations**	
	A. Make and explain inferences	
	B. Support interpretations/conclusions with information from a text	
	C. Make generalizations based on information from a text	
	D. Analyze characters from a story	
VI.	**Recognize points of view, propaganda, and statements of fact and opinion**	
	A. Distinguish fact from opinion in a text	
	B. Identify the author's purpose	
VII.	**Read, analyze, and interpret literature**	
	A. Identify genres of fiction, nonfiction, and poetry	
	B. Identify characteristics representative of a given genre	
	C. Identify important literary elements in a text	
	D. Recognize/interpret figurative language	
VIII.	**Identify and use sources of different types of information**	
	A. Use and interpret graphic sources of information	
	B. Use reference resources and the parts of a book to locate information	
	C. Recognize and use dictionary skills	

Vocabulary

I. Determine the meaning of words in written texts

B. Use context clues to determine word meaning
C. Recognize correct meaning of words with multiple meanings
D. Demonstrate knowledge of synonyms/antonyms/homophones

11

Notes

©ECS Learning Systems, Inc.

Practice 1: Synonyms

Directions: Read the following phrases. Find the word that has the same or about the same meaning as the bolded word. On your answer sheet, darken the circle for the correct word.

1. **foreign** lands

   A familiar
   B absent
   C faraway
   D vague

2. a **license** to drive

   A path
   B permit
   C movement
   D desire

3. **gasp** for breath

   A clasp
   B stop
   C pant
   D scare

4. a **mammoth** building

   A huge
   B hidden
   C attractive
   D small

5. the beautiful **mansion**

   A beast
   B painting
   C castle
   D symbol

6. making **progress**

   A changes
   B products
   C messages
   D improvement

7. the soldiers will **retreat**

   A withdraw
   B escape
   C battle
   D attack

8. a **magnificent** view

   A simple
   B grand
   C cloudy
   D wide

9. the company **logo**

   A business
   B location
   C plan
   D symbol

10. the child's **development**

    A growth
    B behavior
    C question
    D idea

13

Practice 2: Synonyms

Directions: Read the following phrases. Find the word that has the same or about the same meaning as the bolded word. On your answer sheet, darken the circle for the correct word.

1. clam **chowder**

   A sandwich
   B meal
   C bowl
   D stew

2. soft **fabric**

   A voice
   B cushion
   C cloth
   D shoes

3. **investigate** the problem

   A study
   B solve
   C reveal
   D remove

4. a safe **refuge**

   A position
   B decision
   C shelter
   D friend

5. **pronounce** correctly

   A remove
   B say
   C handle
   D review

6. the wild **stallion**

   A rider
   B beast
   C journey
   D horse

7. a **ragged** shirt

   A pressed
   B torn
   C spotted
   D striped

8. with great **glee**

   A anger
   B relief
   C joy
   D sadness

9. **mature** behavior

   A grown-up
   B childish
   C proper
   D difficult

10. a church **hymn**

    A service
    B bench
    C prayer
    D song

14

Practice 3: Synonyms

Directions: Read the following phrases. Find the word that has the same or about the same meaning as the bolded word. On your answer sheet, darken the circle for the correct word.

1. **delay** the trip

   A rush
   B announce
   C seal
   D postpone

2. the necessary **equipment**

   A tools
   B plans
   C drawings
   D places

3. the **frantic** fans

   A repeated
   B excited
   C calm
   D angry

4. **injured** arm

   A bare
   B wounded
   C protected
   D wrapped

5. the **innocent** person

   A guilty
   B careless
   C blameless
   D jealous

6. the shoe **peddler**

   A repairman
   B customer
   C salesman
   D rack

7. a good **profession**

   A career
   B location
   C decision
   D remark

8. **wail** in sorrow

   A sing
   B argue
   C sleep
   D cry

9. **survey** the land

   A purchase
   B inspect
   C remove
   D prepare

10. **unite** the team

    A divide
    B change
    C connect
    D lead

Practice 4: Antonyms

Directions: Read the following phrases. Find the word that has the opposite meaning as the bolded word. On your answer sheet, darken the circle for the correct word.

1. **temporary** home

   A faraway
   B permanent
   C beautiful
   D restored

2. **inherit** the land

   A plow
   B share
   C buy
   D lose

3. **jagged** edges

   A rough
   B broken
   C smooth
   D simple

4. **confess** the truth

   A reveal
   B ask
   C hide
   D admit

5. **peculiar** behavior

   A normal
   B odd
   C calm
   D gentle

6. **select** a partner

   A choose
   B prefer
   C need
   D reject

7. **visible** lines

   A clear
   B hidden
   C obvious
   D straight

8. steady **progress**

   A growth
   B headway
   C retreat
   D movement

9. **murmur** an answer

   A suggest
   B whisper
   C yell
   D sigh

10. complete **misery**

    A pleasure
    B suffering
    C pain
    D envy

Practice 5: Antonyms

Directions: Read the following phrases. Find the word that has the opposite meaning as the bolded word. On your answer sheet, darken the circle for the correct word.

1. you should **proceed**

   A continue
   B follow
   C stop
   D go

2. **renew** the membership

   A begin
   B restart
   C cancel
   D continue

3. **snatch** the ticket

   A release
   B grab
   C lose
   D take

4. **transparent** film

   A clear
   B cloudy
   C cracked
   D direct

5. **precise** answers

   A exact
   B correct
   C forgotten
   D careless

6. **fortunate** person

   A blessed
   B pleased
   C unlucky
   D lost

7. **wholly** to blame

   A usually
   B partly
   C entirely
   D often

8. **fertile** soil

   A fruitful
   B rich
   C heavy
   D barren

9. a time of **strife**

   A peace
   B war
   C decision
   D forgiveness

10. feelings of **rage**

    A anger
    B regret
    C sorrow
    D delight

Practice 6: Antonyms

Directions: Read the following phrases. Find the word that has the opposite meaning as the bolded word. On your answer sheet, darken the circle for the correct word.

1. a **stained** shirt

   A marked
   B colored
   C smudged
   D spotless

2. the team's **triumph**

   A victory
   B defeat
   C schedule
   D location

3. **resent** the offer

   A ignore
   B request
   C appreciate
   D refuse

4. the hero's **tribute**

   A gift
   B praise
   C dishonor
   D success

5. the enemy's **surrender**

   A fight
   B loss
   C regret
   D plan

6. **slump** in the chair

   A droop
   B straighten
   C sag
   D sleep

7. **shrink** the size

   A lessen
   B change
   C remove
   D increase

8. a **jealous** person

   A silly
   B evil
   C trusting
   D resentful

9. **bashful** child

   A bold
   B shy
   C quiet
   D forgetful

10. **blank** page

    A empty
    B white
    C marked
    D missing

Practice 7: Homophones

Directions: Read the following sentences. Choose the word that completes each sentence correctly. On your answer sheet, darken the circle for the correct word.

1. How much money did you
_____ last week?

   A earn
   B urn

2. We will _____ the
voters in our area.

   A pole
   B poll

3. Her _____ voice
bothered him.

   A horse
   B hoarse

4. Do you have a rod and
_____ for fishing?

   A real
   B reel

5. The baby will _____
if you take away her toy.

   A bawl
   B ball

6. Tell _____ we will leave
very soon.

   A hymn
   B him

7. _____ behavior was
better than before.

   A there
   B their

8. The truck will _____ away
the trash.

   A haul
   B hall

9. Can you _____ me
some money?

   A loan
   B lone

10. The old door _____
when you close it.

   A creaks
   B creeks

Practice 8: Homophones

Directions: Read the following sentences. Choose the word that completes each sentence correctly. On your answer sheet, darken the circle for the correct word.

1. How old were you when you learned how to _____ ?

   A serf
   B surf

2. I tried in _____ to buy a ticket to the game.

   A vein
   B vain

3. Do not _____ through the window.

   A peer
   B pier

4. The dress is made from a very _____ fabric.

   A course
   B coarse

5. The _____ smell filled the air.

   A foul
   B fowl

6. Winning the race was quite a_____.

   A feat
   B feet

7. Do you plan to _____ your shirt?

   A dye
   B die

8. Every team in the school deserves _____ treatment.

   A fare
   B fair

9. The _____ on the grass sparkled in the sunlight.

   A due
   B dew

10. My baby brother wanted to eat the _____ cake.

   A hole
   B whole

Practice 9: Homophones

Directions: Read the following sentences. Choose the word that completes each sentence correctly. On your answer sheet, darken the circle for the correct word.

1. You can carry the shells in a small _____ .

   A pale
   B pail

2. I have a _____ in the middle of my back.

   A pain
   B pane

3. My sister does not like to eat any _____.

   A meat
   B meet

4. My mother always tells me that it is not polite to _____ .

   A stair
   B stare

5. I ordered a large salad, a dinner _____ , and a drink.

   A role
   B roll

6. The guest speaker _____ from her chair.

   A rows
   B rose

7. That is my favorite _____ in the whole movie.

   A scene
   B seen

8. The _____ of the flowers filled the room.

   A scent
   B cent

9. How many _____ of hay are in the field?

   A bails
   B bales

10. I need a new _____ of shoes very soon.

    A pair
    B pear

Practice 10: Context Clues

Directions: Read the following sentences. Then choose the best word to fit in the blank. On your answer sheet, darken the circle for the correct word.

1. The police will _____ the crime.

   A injure
   B investigate
   C influence
   D invade

2. Before doing an experiment, you should take special _____.

   A resources
   B surveys
   C precautions
   D awards

3. When I do something wrong, I usually _____ it later.

   A restore
   B disgust
   C regret
   D snatch

4. My parents want to _____ money from their account to mine.

   A transfer
   B develop
   C export
   D operate

5. The teachers served the cake and punch at the _____ for students.

   A committee
   B emergency
   C incident
   D reception

6. The diver saw colorful fish near the coral _____ .

   A refuge
   B frontier
   C scroll
   D reef

7. The little children cry when the older children _____ them.

   A indicate
   B torment
   C whine
   D dispose

8. The teacher said my answer was too _____ and asked for more details.

   A sincere
   B visible
   C vague
   D practical

©ECS Learning Systems, Inc.

22

Practice 11: Context Clues

Directions: Read the following sentences. Then choose the best word to fit in the blank. On your answer sheet, darken the circle for the correct word.

1. We rented a large _____ for the school party.

   A equipment
   B frontier
   C pavilion
   D production

2. Climbing Mt. Everest is always a dangerous _____ .

   A conference
   B expedition
   C continent
   D sacrifice

3. In history class, we studied many ancient _____ .

   A atmospheres
   B civilizations
   C ambitions
   D celebrations

4. I stood on my tiptoes to get a _____ of the President.

   A remark
   B twinkle
   C glimpse
   D vault

5. Your grandparents' _____ did not have all the modern appliances of today.

   A framework
   B reputation
   C impression
   D generation

6. Let's walk to the _____ and look at the ships.

   A wharf
   B plank
   C circuit
   D thicket

7. The student wore the school's _____ on her jacket.

   A license
   B scroll
   C theory
   D emblem

8. Sharon cannot eat the cookies because she is _____ to peanuts.

   A tempted
   B allergic
   C affected
   D mischief

23

Practice 12: Context Clues

Directions: Read the following sentences. Then choose the best word to fit in the blank. On your answer sheet, darken the circle for the correct word.

1. The author wrote a _____ of books about life in other countries.

   A series
   B circuit
   C progress
   D principle

2. My parents were _____ by the clerk's rude behavior.

   A restored
   B assumed
   C calculated
   D stunned

3. In _____ class, the students read about the oceans and rivers of the world.

   A composition
   B geography
   C globe
   D republic

4. I plan my _____ carefully so I can buy what I need.

   A resource
   B notion
   C conference
   D budget

5. During the hike, our boots were ruined because we had to _____ through the mud.

   A scuff
   B clog
   C trudge
   D delay

6. The children waded in the creek and caught _____ in their pails.

   A hulls
   B minnows
   C swarms
   D crests

7. Please _____ the answer by circling the correct letter.

   A indicate
   B remark
   C fulfill
   D confess

8. At his office, John is expected to act in a _____ way.

   A foreign
   B temporary
   C professional
   D gleeful

Practice 13: Multiple-Meaning Words

Directions: Read each pair of sentences. Find the word that completes both sentences. On your answer sheet, darken the circle for the correct word.

1. In this _____ , I think you are right.

   Buy a _____ of soft drinks.

   A position
   B time
   C case
   D crate

2. My parents play _____ with their friends.

   The city built a new _____ across the river.

   A bridge
   B span
   C cards
   D line

3. Mrs. Alva works at an important law _____ .

   The mattress was _____, not soft.

   A company
   B field
   C firm
   D solid

4. The children enjoyed their day at the _____ .

   In fairy tales, the princess is usually young and _____ .

   A kind
   B fair
   C shore
   D lovely

5. Plant the seeds deep in the _____ .

   We _____ the coffee beans at the store.

   A pot
   B soil
   C bought
   D ground

6. _____ the ladder against the wall.

   I only eat _____ meat.

   A tilt
   B plain
   C set
   D lean

Practice 14: Multiple-Meaning Words

Directions: Read each pair of sentences. Find the word that completes both sentences. On your answer sheet, darken the circle for the correct word.

1. The lemonade filled the _____ .

   After the game, the _____ talked to the reporters.

   A player
   B pitcher
   C fan
   D team

2. My friend likes to _____ me on the arm.

   I lost one _____ in the washing machine.

   A towel
   B pinch
   C tap
   D sock

3. We led the horse into his _____ .

   We tried to _____ for more time.

   A shed
   B stable
   C stall
   D barn

4. The lemons were too _____ to eat.

   I ate an apple _____ for dessert.

   A sour
   B crisp
   C tart
   D slice

5. How deep is that _____ ?

   Last week I didn't feel _____ .

   A pit
   B well
   C hole
   D ill

6. Did you see the _____ at the zoo?

   The heat is so hard to _____ .

   A bear
   B take
   C beast
   D crowd

26

Practice 15: Multiple-Meaning Words

Directions: Read each question. Find the word that fits both bolded meanings. On your answer sheet, darken the circle for the correct word.

1. Which word means **the end** and **continue**?

    A rear
    B final
    C last
    D go

2. Which word means **part of the sea** and **howl**?

    A bay
    B gulf
    C cove
    D cry

3. Which word means a **black bird** and a **rooster's cry**?

    A caw
    B raven
    C screech
    D crow

4. Which word means **not heavy** and **not dark**?

    A small
    B bright
    C light
    D open

5. Which word means **quite smart** and **not dark**?

    A tops
    B bright
    C light
    D brain

6. Which word means **part of a guitar** and **worry**?

    A ridge
    B fret
    C neck
    D string

7. Which word means **average** and **not nice**?

    A even
    B kind
    C mean
    D pain

8. Which word means a **piece of paper** and **escape**?

    A strip
    B shred
    C skip
    D slip

Practice 16: Analogies

Directions: Read each analogy. Find the word that correctly completes each analogy. On your answer sheet, darken the circle for the correct word.

1. **Reading** is to **library** as **exercise** is to _____ .

   A outside
   B running
   C gymnasium
   D behavior

2. **Tall** is to **mountain** as **deep** is to _____ .

   A hillside
   B ravine
   C sink
   D slope

3. **Foods** are to **cupboard** as **crates** are to _____ .

   A room
   B theater
   C warehouse
   D patio

4. **Adult** is to **youngster** as **tree** is to _____ .

   A branch
   B blossom
   C cabinet
   D sapling

5. **Cow** is to **beef** as **deer** is to _____ .

   A venison
   B mutton
   C chicken
   D stew

6. **Loss** is to **defeat** as **victory** is to _____ .

   A tragedy
   B triumph
   C retreat
   D marvelous

7. **Air** is to **parachute** as **water** is to _____ .

   A coast
   B diver
   C arch
   D snorkel

8. **Fish** are to **school** as **bees** are to _____ .

   A clasp
   B sting
   C swarm
   D class

Practice 17: Analogies

Directions: Read each analogy. Find the word that correctly completes each analogy. On your answer sheet, darken the circle for the correct word.

1. **Gloves** are to **hands** as _____ are to **eyes**.

   A eyelashes
   B sight
   C clothes
   D goggles

2. **Fry** is to **hamburger** as _____ is to **soup**.

   A cover
   B sip
   C simmer
   D stir

3. **Teacher** is to **education** as **farmer** is to _____.

   A science
   B agriculture
   C geography
   D crops

4. **Yellow** is to **color** as _____ is to **shape**.

   A rotate
   B circular
   C building
   D movement

5. **Skyscraper** is to **house** as _____ is to **pebble**.

   A boulder
   B ground
   C stone
   D heavy

6. **Bounce** is to **ball** as **spin** is to _____.

   A tool
   B change
   C globe
   D circle

7. **Spear** is to **hunter** as _____ is to **soldier**.

   A field
   B attack
   C musket
   D warfare

8. **Large** is to **small** as _____ is to **young**.

   A childish
   B simple
   C junior
   D mature

29

Practice 18: Analogies

Directions: Read each analogy. Find the word that correctly completes each analogy. On your answer sheet, darken the circle for the correct word.

1. **Produce** is to **production** as **tempt** is to _____ .

   A tempting
   B temptation
   C problem
   D commotion

2. **Regret** is to **sorrow** as _____ is to **happiness**.

   A resist
   B upset
   C marvelous
   D rejoice

3. **Moon** is to **shining** as **star** is to _____ .

   A gazing
   B falling
   C twinkling
   D treating

4. **Pastor** is to **church** as **professor** is to _____ .

   A instruction
   B position
   C university
   D composition

5. **Tablecloth** is to **table** as _____ is to **lap**.

   A napkin
   B chair
   C sitting
   D crumbs

6. **Student** is to **class** as **member** is to _____ .

   A individual
   B learning
   C committee
   D leader

7. **Sketch** is to **drawing** as _____ is to **writing**.

   A vision
   B composition
   C pencil
   D equipment

8. **Drive** is to **automobile** as _____ is to **machine**.

   A steer
   B order
   C produce
   D operate

Comprehension

I. Determine the meaning of words in written texts

    A. Use root words and other structural cues to recognize new words
    B. Use context clues to determine word meaning
    C. Recognize correct meaning of words with multiple meanings
    D. Demonstrate knowledge of synonyms and antonyms

II. Identify supporting ideas

    A. Identify relevant facts and details
    B. Sequence events in chronological order
    C. Follow written directions
    D. Identify the importance of setting to a story's meaning

III. Summarize a variety of written texts

    A. Determine the main idea or essential message of a text
    B. Summarize the major ideas, themes, or procedures in a text

IV. Perceive relationships and recognize outcomes

    A. Identify cause and effect relationships in a text
    B. Make and verify predictions with information from a text
    C. Identify similarities and differences in text(s)

V. Analyze information in order to make inferences and generalizations

    A. Make and explain inferences
    B. Support interpretations/conclusions with information from a text
    C. Make generalizations based on information from a text
    D. Analyze characters from a story

VI. Recognize points of view, propaganda, and statements of fact and opinion

    A. Distinguish fact from opinion in a text
    B. Identify the author's purpose

VII. Determine the meaning of words in written texts

    A. Identify genres of fiction, nonfiction, and poetry
    B. Identify characteristics representative of a given genre
    C. Identify important literary elements in a text

Notes

1: A Helpful Little Lady

In China, people call them "flower ladies." People in Europe may call them "little fatties." You may know them as "ladybugs" or "lady beetles." Whatever you call them, these small, round insects are important friends to people around the world.

All Kinds of Ladybugs

Ladybugs are small beetles. Like all beetles, they are insects. There are more than 3,000 kinds of ladybugs in the world. In this country, there are more than 100 kinds. Each **kind** is a little different from the others.

All ladybugs are small. The largest kind is no more than one-third to one-half inch long. Some kinds are even smaller than that—maybe less than one-tenth inch long.

You may be most familiar with the small, red ladybug with seven black spots. Ladybugs actually come in many colors, such as orange, yellow, and black. Some have no markings on their outer, colored shells. However, most **varieties** have black spots or patches. Some ladybugs have two spots. Others have five or seven spots. Some of these little beetles have more than 20 spots on their backs!

All ladybugs have hard shells on their bodies. The shells are called **elytra**. These outer coverings look like wings, but they are not. The elytra cover and protect the ladybug's "flying" wings.

The flying wings are much longer and thinner than the hard shells. When a ladybug wants to fly, it lifts the hard shells and spreads its wings. Then it takes off!

Warning: Stay Away

Like most animals, the ladybug must protect itself from enemies. Its first **defense** is its color. Its color can blend in with its surroundings. This makes the ladybug hard to see. The colorful markings also warn enemies, such as ants and birds, that ladybugs taste bad. A ladybug protects itself in another way, too. It can release a bad-smelling liquid through its legs. This is called reflex bleeding. The bad smell tells the ladybug's enemies to "stay away."

The Ladybug's Diet

A ladybug is no "lady" when it comes to eating. Every ladybug has a huge appetite. One adult ladybug can eat more than 50 insects in one day! Ladybugs eat many kinds of insects, too. They eat spider mites and scale bugs. A ladybug's favorite meal is the aphid.

The ladybug's diet makes it a friend to farmers and gardeners. It eats many insects that destroy crops. For example, **aphids**, or plant lice, live on plants and suck food from them. This can kill the plants. To protect their plants, many growers let ladybugs loose in their fields and gardens. The ladybugs eat the unwanted guests. In some places, people even have ladybug farms. They raise ladybugs and sell them to growers who need them.

Ladybugs are helpful members of the insect world. If one lands on your shoulder, take a close look at it. You might also say, "Thanks for your help, little lady."

Context Clues (I.B)
1. In this passage, the word **varieties** means—

A insects
B ladybugs
C spots
D kinds

Context Clues (I.B)
2. What does the word **elytra** mean in this passage?

A A ladybug's true wings
B The spots on a ladybug's back
C Outer coverings that protect a ladybug's wings
D A ladybug's enemy

Synonyms/Antonyms (I.D)
3. Which word means about the same thing as **defense**?

A Color
B Surroundings
C Protection
D Markings

Context Clues (I.B)
4. In this passage, the word **aphids** means—

A plant lice
B farmers and gardeners
C ladybug farms
D unwanted insects

Multiple-Meaning Words (I.C)
5. In this passage, the word **kind** means—

A nice
B type
C sort out
D brand name

Facts/Details (II.A)
6. How many kinds of ladybugs are in the world?

A 20
B 50
C 100
D 3,000

Facts/Details (II.A)
7. Reflex bleeding is how a ladybug—

A blends in with its surroundings
B makes colorful markings
C makes a smell to keep its enemies away
D lifts its wings

Sequential Order (II.B)

8. In order to fly, a ladybug must first—

A release liquid from its legs
B lift its hard shell
C have at least seven spots
D protect itself from enemies

Summarize Ideas/Themes (III.B)

9. Which is the best summary of the sixth paragraph?

A Ladybugs can blend in with their surroundings.
B Ladybugs have several ways to protect themselves from their enemies.
C Ladybugs are interesting and useful insects.
D Ants and birds do not like the taste of ladybugs.

Cause/Effect (IV.A)

10. Some farmers release ladybugs in their fields in order to—

A give ladybugs a good diet
B raise ladybugs and sell them to other farmers
C make the surroundings more beautiful and interesting
D get rid of insects that destroy crops

Fact/Opinion (VI.A)

11. Which is a FACT in this passage?

A In China, people call ladybugs "little fatties."
B Ladybugs can come in many different colors.
C Ladybugs are the most important insects in the world.
D Everyone in the world likes to look at ladybugs.

Interpretations/Conclusions (V.B)

12. Ladybugs are helpful to farmers because they—

A add color to the crops
B do not kill plants
C eat insects that destroy crops
D defend themselves from other insects

Generalizations (V.C)

13. Which word would most farmers probably use to describe ladybugs?

A Dangerous
B Helpful
C Colorful
D Unwanted

Genre Characteristics (VII.B)

14. This passage would most likely be found in a—

A book of poetry
B collection of folk tales
C science magazine
D dictionary

Facts/Details (II.A)

15. Complete the diagram below by listing facts and details from the passage that support the main idea written in the circle.

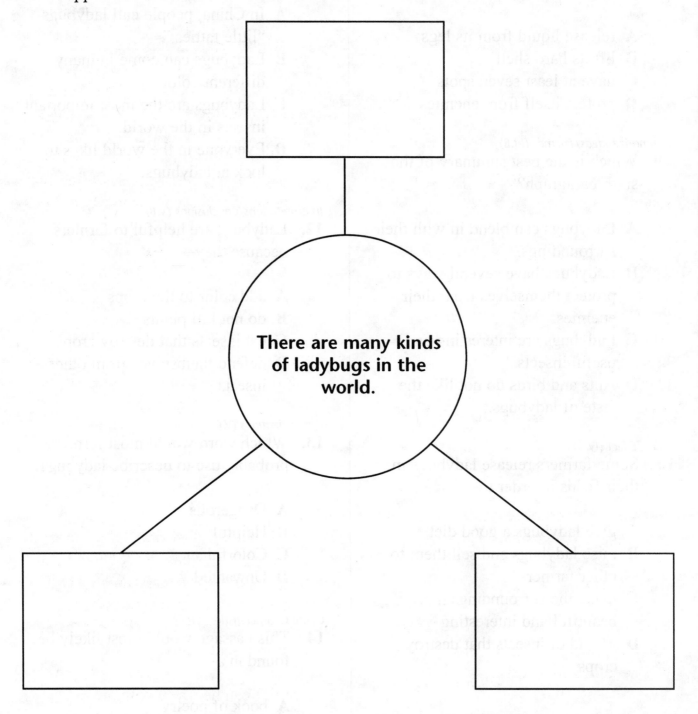

36

2: A New Way to Study

Do you know how to study? One easy way to study is called SQ3R. SQ3R stands for five simple steps—

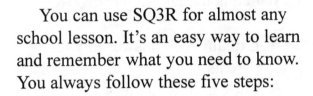

- Survey
- Question
- Read
- Recite
- Review

You can use SQ3R for almost any school lesson. It's an easy way to learn and remember what you need to know. You always follow these five steps:

1. Survey the lesson or information that you want to study. Look over the whole assignment before you begin. Try to get a good idea about the work you must do.

If you will be reading, look over the whole passage. Look at the beginning, middle, and end. Look at the pictures, graphs, and charts. Are there questions at the end? If there are, you should read them, too. The questions can show you what the lesson is about.

If you will be writing, do the same kind of survey. Look at the questions you must answer. Figure out what you will need to know at the end.

2. Ask yourself some questions about your assignment. Make up questions from the headings, titles, and pictures. For example, you could make up a question about the passage you are

reading now— "How do I use the SQ3R study method?"

Write your questions on paper. Use them to guide your reading and studying. Your teacher may give you questions. You should use them to guide your reading, too.

3. Read (or write) your assignment. Think about the questions from step two. Use them to guide your work. Look for the answers to the questions.

4. It is time to **recite**. After you finish the third step, answer the questions from step two. If you have written answers, read over your work. Make sure you have answered what was asked. Your mom, dad, or older brother or sister can ask you questions about your work, too. This is a good time to **summarize** the work in your own words. Can you explain the main ideas of your work?

5. Review your work. Think about it one more time. What was it about? Did you finish the whole assignment? Did you answer all your questions? You might summarize your work by writing one or two sentences.

SQ3R can help you with any assignment. It will also help you be a more **independent** reader and learner. You will feel good about working on your own. You will learn how to guide your own school work. You will probably become a better student. SQ3R is a study tool you can use throughout your life.

Synonyms/Antonyms (I.D)

1. Which word means about the same as the word **survey**?

   A Finish
   B Write
   C Scan
   D Remember

Context Clues (I.B)

2. What does the word **recite** mean in this passage?

   A Give the answers
   B Stop studying
   C Write or read
   D Help someone

Context Clues (I.B)

3. In this passage, the word **summarize** means—

   A use many details
   B ask for help
   C present main ideas in a few words
   D take a rest

Structural Cues (I.A)

4. In this passage, the word **independent** means—

   A needing help from others
   B able to work alone
   C slow and careful
   D interesting

Sequential Order (II.B)

5. Which is the last step of SQ3R?

   A Explain each answer to your parents
   B Look at how the lesson is organized
   C Write your questions on paper
   D Look over your work at least one time

Follow Directions (II.C)

6. You should look over the questions before you begin an assignment because—

   A this is the only way to answer them
   B they can show you what the lesson is about
   C this will make you more independent
   D this is the fastest way to work

Main Idea (III.A)

7. This passage is mostly about—

   A the best way to get better grades
   B answering questions correctly
   C how to use SQ3R to study
   D how to improve your grades

Cause/Effect (IV.A)

8. According to the passage, if you make up your own questions, then you will—

A learn more
B waste too much time
C make your teacher happy
D know what the assignment is

Predictions (IV.B)

9. What will probably happen if you learn and use SQ3R?

A You will earn all A's on your report card.
B Your teacher will give you more work to do.
C You will become a better student.
D You will spend less time on school work.

Fact/Opinion (VI.A)

10. Which is an OPINION in this passage?

A The first step in SQ3R is to survey.
B SQ3R is an easy way to learn and remember.
C Reading is part of the SQ3R method.
D SQ3R has five steps.

Author's Purpose (VI.B)

11. Why did the author write this passage?

A To prove how little students know about studying
B To show students one useful way to study
C To entertain students who were tired of studying
D To prove that students have too much school work

Inferences (V.A)

12. From the information the author gives in this passage, you could conclude that the SQ3R method of studying is—

A complicated
B worthless
C effective
D entertaining

Identify Genres (VII.A)

13. "A New Way to Study" is mostly a(n)—

A personal narrative
B set of directions
C comparison and contrast
D interview

Interpretations/Conclusions (V.B)

14. The author of this passage believes that SQ3R is a good way to study. Do you agree or disagree? Write a letter to the author and explain why you agree or disagree with her. Use information from the passage in your answer.

Similarities/Differences (IV.C)

15. Think about the way you study. How is your study method like the SQ3R method? How is your study method different from the SQ3R method? Organize your ideas in the Venn diagram below.

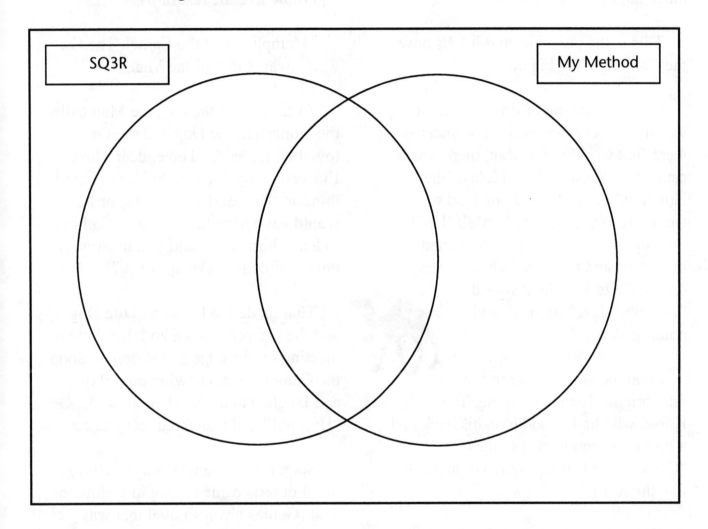

SQ3R

My Method

3: How the Camel Got His Hump

Rudyard Kipling wrote a series of tales called "Just So Stories." The following story is a retelling of one of those tales.

This is the next tale, and it tells how the Camel got his big hump.

In the beginning of time, when the world was very new and the animals were first working for Man, there was a camel that lived in the middle of the Howling Desert. He did not want to work. He was a Howler himself. He did nothing but eat sticks and thorns and milkweed and prickles. Whenever any-one spoke to him, he just said "Humph!" Just "Humph" and nothing else.

Soon the Horse came to him on a bright Monday morning. The Horse, who had a saddle on his back and a bit in his mouth, said to the Camel, "Camel, dear Camel, come out and trot like the rest of us!"

"Humph!" said the Camel. The Horse went away and told the Man.

Soon the Dog came up to the Camel. The Dog, who had a stick in his mouth, said to the Camel, "Camel, dear Camel, come and **fetch** and carry like the rest of us."

"Humph!" said the Camel. The Dog went away and told the Man.

Then the Ox, with a **yoke** on his neck, came around to meet the Camel. The Ox said, "Camel, dear Camel, come and plow like the rest of us."

"Humph!" said the Camel. The Ox went away and told the Man.

At the end of the day, the Man called the Horse and the Dog and the Ox together. He said, "Three, dear Three, I'm very sorry for you, but that Humph-thing in the desert can't work, or he would have been here by now. So I am to leave him alone, and you must work double-time to make up for it."

That made the Horse and the Dog and the Ox very angry, and they held a meeting on the edge of the desert. Soon the Camel came, chewing on milkweed, and laughed at them. Then he said "Humph!" and wandered away again.

Soon the Genie who was in **charge** of all deserts came rolling in a cloud of dust (Genies always travel that way because it is Magic). He stopped at the meeting of the Horse and the Dog and the Ox.

"Genie of all deserts," said the Horse, "is it right for any one to be **idle**, while the rest of us are working so hard? There is so much to do with the world being new and all."

"Certainly not," said the Genie.

"Well," said the Horse, "there's a thing in the middle of your Howling Desert—he's a Howler himself—with a long neck and long legs. He hasn't done a bit of work since Monday morning. He won't trot."

"Oh my," said the Genie, "that's my Camel! What does he say about it?"

"He says 'Humph!'" said the Dog. "He won't fetch and carry!"

"Does he say anything else?" asked the Genie.

"Only 'Humph!'" said the Ox. "He won't plow."

"Very well," said the Genie. "I'll humph him if you will kindly wait just a minute."

The Genie rolled himself up in his dust cloak and took off across the desert. He found the Camel doing nothing but looking at his own **reflection** in a pool of water.

"My long and bubbling friend," said the Genie, "what do I hear about your doing no work?"

"Humph!" said the Camel.

The Genie sat down, his chin in his hand, and began to think while the Camel continued to look at his own reflection in the pool of water.

"You've given the Horse and the Dog and the Ox extra work because you are so lazy," said the Genie.

"Humph!" said the Camel.

"I wouldn't say that again if I were you," said the Genie. "You might say it once too often. Bubbles, I want you to work."

The Camel just said "Humph!" again. But no sooner had he said it than he saw his back, which he was so proud of, puffing up and puffing up into a great huge humph.

"Do you see that?" asked the Genie. "That's your very own humph that you've brought upon yourself by not working. Today is Thursday, and you've done no work since Monday, when the work began. Now you are going to work."

"How can I," said the Camel, "with this humph on my back?"

"That's the reason for the humph on your back," said the Genie. "You did not work for three days. Now you can work for three days without eating because you can live on your humph. Don't ever say I never did anything for you. Come out of the desert and find the Three, and begin to do your share of the work."

And the Camel humphed himself, humph and all, and went away to join the Three. And from that day to this, the Camel always wears a humph (although we call it a 'hump' so we don't hurt his feelings), but he has never caught up with the three days he missed at the beginning of the world—and he has never learned how to behave!

Synonyms/Antonyms (I.D)

1. Which word means about the same as the word **fetch**?

A Remove
B Choose
C Bring
D Tell

Context Clues (I.B)

2. In this passage, the word **yoke** means—

A neck
B harness
C rope
D plow

Context Clues (I.B)

3. The word **idle** means—

A useful
B angry
C careless
D lazy

Structural Cues (I.A)

4. Which word is the root word of **reflection**?

A Flee
B Elect
C Reflect
D Reflecting

Multiple Meanings (I.C)

5. In this passage, the word **charge** means—

A command
B load
C blame
D rush

Facts/Details (II.A)

6. Which character gives the Camel his hump?

A The Horse
B The Genie
C The Dog
D The Man

Sequential Order (II.B)

7. When do the Horse, the Dog, and the Ox meet at the edge of the desert?

A After the Genie arrives at the desert
B Before they meet the Camel for the first time
C After the Camel gets his hump
D After the Man tells them they must work double time

Setting (II.D)

8. Where does the Genie find the Camel?

A At the edge of the desert
B In the desert with the other animals
C Near a pool of water
D At the Man's home

Summarize Ideas/Themes (III.B)

9. Which of the following is the best summary of this passage?

A A lazy animal escapes from the desert.
B Three animals learn how to work together and help people.
C An animal is punished for being lazy and forced to do his share of the work.
D A genie performs magic to help animals in the desert.

Cause/Effect (IV.A)

10. The Camel upsets the other animals because he—

A stares at his own reflection
B refuses to do his share of work
C grows a hump on his back
D does not attend their meeting

Inferences (V.A)

11. The animals have a lot of work to do because the—

A Man is unkind to them
B Genie is coming to visit
C Camel has made such a mess
D world is new

Character Analysis (V.D)

12. Which word best describes how the Horse, the Dog, and the Ox feel toward the Camel?

A Resentful
B Understanding
C Frightened
D Uninterested

Author's Purpose (VI.B)

13. The author probably wrote this passage in order to—

A explain why Camels live in the desert
B entertain readers with a funny tale
C describe how animals work for man
D convince readers that camels are lazy animals

Figurative Language (VII.D)

14. In this passage, animals can talk. This is an example of—

A a metaphor
B personification
C exaggeration
D conflict

Similarities/Differences (IV.C)

15. Choose one of these characters: the Genie or the Camel. Explain how this character is similar to a character you remember from another story. Use specific details in your answer.

_____

_____

_____

_____

_____

_____

_____

_____

_____

_____

_____

_____

_____

_____

Summarize Ideas/Themes (III.B)

16. A theme is the main message of a passage. What is the theme of this passage? Use information from the passage in your answer.

_____

_____

_____

_____

_____

_____

_____

_____

_____

_____

_____

_____

_____

4: Giants of the Desert

The saguaro cactus is a large plant that grows only in the Sonoran Desert. When fully grown, it can stand 50 feet tall and weigh as much as 10 tons. This cactus is big, but it has other interesting features, too.

How the Saguaro Cactus Begins

The saguaro cactus begins as a tiny, black seed. Its fruit can make more than 1,000 seeds. The seeds are hard to see because they are so small.

Birds and other desert animals eat the saguaro's fruit. The birds **ingest** the seeds with the fruit. As they travel around the desert, the animals leave the seeds in their droppings. In this way, a seed can travel far away from the parent tree.

A saguaro cactus grows best in rocky soil that holds moisture and protects it from the wind. Rocky soil also gives the seed a good place to hide from animals that might eat it. If it is too hot or too cold, the seed will not survive. It must have the right amount of rain and sunshine. When everything is right, the seed will sprout.

The young saguaro cactus, called a **seedling**, grows best under the shade and protection of a larger plant. The larger plant protects the seedling from sun, wind, and animals. The seedling also needs just the right growing conditions. Too much rain can wash it away. Too little rain will kill it.

How the Saguaro Cactus Grows

The saguaro cactus grows slowly. After two years, the plant will be less than one inch tall. After 10 years, it may be six inches tall. When it is 50 years old, it will be 6 to 10 feet tall and have one main branch. A saguaro cactus does not have its first **arms** until it is 35 to 50 years old. Some saguaro cacti can live to be 200 years old. These giants are much older than the people who come to see them!

Most plants use their roots to hold them **upright**. A saguaro cactus cannot do this. Its roots are not deep enough. The roots can stretch more than 50 feet from the plant and let the cactus absorb more water when it rains, but they cannot support the plant's weight and height. The saguaro cactus uses its **core** to hold it upright. The core runs through the center of the cactus. The core has several wooden rods that stretch from the base of the cactus to the top. The rods hold the cactus in place and support its soft, outer part. The outer part stores water and can weigh several thousand pounds. When the cactus dies, the soft part rots away, but the wooden rods remain. Small creatures, such as birds and insects, make their homes in the rods.

Each spring, the saguaro cactus blooms in lovely white flowers. Unlike other flowering plants, it blooms at night! In the morning, the flowers dry and wither in the hot sun. The flowers make a red, juicy fruit that is a favorite food for many desert animals. Even people like this fruit. The Papago Indians make syrup and wine from the fruit. Of course, the fruit makes the plant's seeds, too—and the giant plant's life cycle begins again.

The desert's hot, dry climate makes it hard for the saguaro cactus to survive. Yet, it manages to live and make a place for itself. It is a true survivor in the desert world!

Context Clues (I.B)

1. The word **ingest** means—

    A hide
    B leave
    C make
    D take in

Structural Cues (I.A)

2. What does the word **seedling** mean in this passage?

    A A large plant
    B Young saguaro cactus
    C Protection
    D Growing condition

Context Clues (I.B)

3. The word **core** means—

    A the root of a saguaro cactus
    B the outer part of a saguaro cactus
    C the base of a saguaro cactus
    D the wooden center of a saguaro cactus

Multiple-Meaning Words (I.C)

4. What does the word **arms** mean in this passage?

    A Parts of the human body
    B Weapons
    C Side bars of a chair
    D Branches of a plant

Synonyms/Antonyms (I.D)

5. Which of the following words means the OPPOSITE of **upright**?

    A Straight
    B Bent
    C Vertical
    D Linear

Facts/Details (II.A)

6. At what age does a saguaro cactus reach its full height?

    A 150 years
    B 50 years
    C 10 years
    D 2 years

Sequential Order (II.B)

7. A saguaro cactus grows its first arm—

    A right after it sprouts
    B when it is two years old
    C just before it is fully grown
    D when it is 10 years old

Main Idea (III.A)

8. This passage is mostly about how—

A the saguaro cactus looks and grows

B people use the saguaro cactus

C a saguaro cactus grows its arms

D a saguaro cactus uses its core

Cause/Effect (IV.A)

9. The roots of a saguaro cactus can not hold it upright because—

A the roots do not stretch

B the roots are not deep enough to support such a large plant

C the core of the saguaro cactus supports the plant

D the roots absorb too much water when it rains

Inferences (V.A)

10. You can tell from the passage that—

A a saguaro cactus can grow almost anywhere

B most saguaro cactus seeds grow to be full size plants

C a saguaro cactus seed needs special conditions to sprout and grow

D desert animals only eat fruit from the saguaro cactus

Generalizations (V.C)

11. You can tell from information in this passage that both desert animals and people find the saguaro cactus to be—

A dangerous

B wet

C useful

D worthless

Fact/Opinion (VI.A)

12. Which is an OPINION in the passage?

A A saguaro cactus fruit can make 1,000 seeds.

B A saguaro cactus can live to be 200 years old.

C The core of a saguaro cactus holds it upright.

D The saguaro cactus has interesting features.

Genre Characteristics (VII.B)

13. This passage might be included in a science magazine because it—

A gives factual information about a desert plant

B includes a picture of a saguaro cactus

C is divided into sections and paragraphs

D shows how the Papago Indians use the saguaro cactus

Similarities/Differences (IV.C)

14. Think of a tree that grows near your home. How is the tree similar to the saguaro cactus? How is the tree different from the saguaro cactus? Write two paragraphs about the tree and saguaro cactus. In the first paragraph, explain how they are similar. In the second paragraph, explain how they are different. Use information from the passage in your answer.

5: A New Look at Old Maps

Maps from the Past

Have you ever used a map? Some people use maps to find places. Others use maps to plan a vacation or check the weather.

People use maps for other reasons, too. For example, some people like to study maps from the past. They want maps that show what places looked like many years ago. These are called **historical maps**. These are probably the most interesting maps to use.

Some historical maps are not really old. Workers at map companies study famous places or events from long ago. Then they make maps that show important places from the past. The maps might show battlefields, old roads, or towns. People can buy these maps and study them.

Other historical maps are very old. They have lasted for a long time. For example, we still have a few maps made by famous explorers. These maps are hundreds of years old. As you might expect, it is easy to **damage** old maps. We keep many of them in libraries, museums, or government offices. These are safe places for old maps.

Using Old Maps

Why would anyone want or need old maps? Some people just like to look at them. Old maps can show how a place grew and developed. You can see where people built their homes or businesses.

If you like history, this information is interesting. Other people find old maps useful in some way. For example, old maps sometimes show who once owned land in an area. You could use these maps to learn about family members from the past.

How to Find Old Maps

You can find historical maps in many different places. Many groups keep a library of old maps. The public library usually has a list of these groups. State and local governments also may keep important papers such as old maps. You might find an old map in your city's **archive**. An archive is a library for important papers.

You can learn many things from old maps. Finding the right map may take work, but the work can pay off.

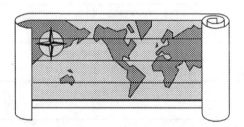

Context Clues (I.B)

1. In this passage, the term **historical maps** means—

   A very old maps
   B maps that show how places looked long ago
   C maps used for vacations
   D weather maps

Context Clues (I.B)

2. In this passage, the word **archive** means—

   A government papers
   B public library
   C library for important papers
   D museum

Synonyms/Antonyms (I.D)

3. Which word means about the same as the word **damage**?

   A Preserve
   B Study
   C Purchase
   D Harm

Structural Cues (I.A)

4. What is the root of the word **historical**?

   A Historian
   B Story
   C History
   D His

Facts/ Details (II.A)

5. According to the passage, where could you find a list of groups that keep a library of old maps?

   A At an archive
   B In a public library
   C In a museum
   D At a government office

Main Idea (III.A)

6. What is the main idea of the **fifth** paragraph of this passage?

   A Old maps show how places grow.
   B Old maps are interesting.
   C People like to look at old maps.
   D People want old maps for different reasons.

Cause/Effect (IV.A)

7. Many historical maps are kept in libraries and museums because—

   A people will not find them there
   B the maps will be safe there
   C people do not want to buy them
   D some towns do not have libraries

Inferences (V.A)

8. Map companies make maps that show important places from the past because—

   A they want to replace maps that are very old
   B there are more old maps available
   C the government asked them to make the maps
   D people use these maps to learn about the past

Fact/Opinion (VI.A)

9. Which of these is an OPINION in this passage?

A People use maps to plan vacations.

B Historical maps may be kept in government offices.

C Historical maps are the most interesting maps to use.

D Some old maps show who once owned pieces of land.

Author's Purpose (VI.B)

10. The author probably wrote this passage to—

A encourage readers to buy old maps

B explain different uses for old maps

C explain how old maps can be saved

D express personal interest in old maps

Identify Genres (VII.A); Genre Characteristics (VII.B)

11. Is this passage fiction or nonfiction? How do you know? Use information from the passage in your answer.

_____

_____

_____

_____

_____

_____

_____

_____

6: The Big Bear-Cats of China

 A giant panda is a cute animal, but what is it? Its scientific name means "black and white." Some people call the animal a "panda," which means "bamboo eater." In China, people call it a "big bear-cat." For many years, people thought the panda was a bear because it looked like a bear. Other scientists thought the panda was more like a raccoon. After years of study, scientists now think that the giant panda may be a bear after all. No one really knows for sure.

At birth, a baby panda weighs about three ounces and is about six inches long. It is covered with very fine hair. The tiny cub is also blind. After 18 months, it leaves its mother and lives on its own. An adult panda is about five feet tall. An adult male weighs about 250 pounds.

The giant panda lives in the mountains of southwest China. These mountains have bamboo forests. Bamboo is the panda's favorite food. A panda spends more than half the day eating bamboo. Most adult pandas eat 35 to 45 pounds of bamboo daily, but some can eat as much as 75 pounds in a day.

Bamboo is not really a good food. A giant panda can only digest about one-tenth of the bamboo it eats, so it must eat large amounts of bamboo to live. A panda can eat other kinds of food. In zoos, its diet may include carrots, apples, and rice.

The giant panda has many special features that help it live. For example, a thick fur protects the panda from the cold, damp climate of the mountains. The fur **repels** water and keeps the animal dry. The panda also has a long wrist bone that it uses like a thumb. The giant panda is a great climber, too. It can quickly **scale** a tree to escape from its enemies. The panda's good hearing lets it find enemies that it cannot see.

The giant panda has lived on earth for millions of years. Today, fewer than 1,000 pandas live in the wild. About 100 pandas live in zoos around the world. Why are there so few giant pandas left on the earth? There are many reasons. Much of the animal's **habitat** has been destroyed. People have moved closer and closer and taken the panda's land. Hunting and trapping also have **reduced** the panda population. The bamboo forests have started to die. Now there is less food for the giant panda.

People around the world know that giant pandas are in danger. The Chinese government has built several protected areas for the animals. The government also punishes people who kill or capture giant pandas. Many zoos have programs to save the giant pandas. If people work together, maybe they can save the "big bear-cats" of China.

Context Clues (I.B)
1. In this passage, the word **repels** means—

    A attracts
    B wets
    C pulls in
    D keeps away

Multiple-Meanings (I.C)
2. In this passage, the word **scale** means—

    A musical notes
    B a weighing device
    C climb
    D part of a fish

Context Clues (I.B)
3. The word **habitat** means—

    A bamboo
    B zoo
    C natural home
    D earth

Synonyms/Antonyms (I.D)
4. Which word means about the same as the word **reduced**?

    A Lowered
    B Saved
    C Increased
    D Covered

Facts/Details (II.A)
5. According to the passage, about how much does a baby panda weigh at birth?

    A 35 pounds
    B 3 pounds
    C 18 ounces
    D 3 ounces

Facts/Details (II.A)
6. Which of the following is the panda's favorite food?

    A Carrots
    B Bamboo
    C Apples
    D Rice

Sequential Order (II.B)
7. A panda cub leaves its mother—

    A when it is five feet tall
    B right after its birth
    C after 18 months
    D after three years

Main Idea (III.A)
8. The **fifth** paragraph in this passage is mostly about—

    A how the giant panda's fur repels water
    B the climate where the giant panda lives
    C special features that help the giant panda live
    D the giant panda's daily diet

Cause/Effect (IV.A)

9. The giant panda stays dry in the damp mountains because—

A its fur protects it from water
B it can climb trees easily
C it is drier in the bamboo forests
D its diet protects it from the rain

Predictions (IV.B)

10. Based on information in this passage, the Chinese government most likely will—

A capture the giant pandas and put them in zoos
B look for new ways to protect the giant pandas
C end all programs to protect the giant pandas
D encourage people to move closer to the country's bamboo forests

Generalizations (V.C)

11. You can tell from the passage that the giant panda's future—

A is not possible
B does not matter to people
C will be easy
D is not certain

Inferences (V.A)

12. The giant pandas are in great danger today because—

A the Chinese government built protected areas for the animals
B they live in a cold, damp climate
C their home was not protected in the past
D zoos do not feed the animals the right food

Fact/Opinion (VI.A)

13. Which is an OPINION from the passage?

A A giant panda is a cute animal.
B The giant panda lives in the mountains of southwest China.
C Adult pandas eat 35-45 pounds of bamboo each day.
D The giant panda uses its wrist bone like a thumb.

Author's Purpose (VI.B)

14. The author probably wrote this passage in order to—

A convince readers that pandas should live in zoos
B show readers how funny giant pandas can be
C teach readers about the giant pandas and the problems they face
D provide solutions for the problems faced by giant pandas

Facts/Details (II.A)
15. Complete the diagram below by listing facts and details from the passage that support the main idea written in the circle.

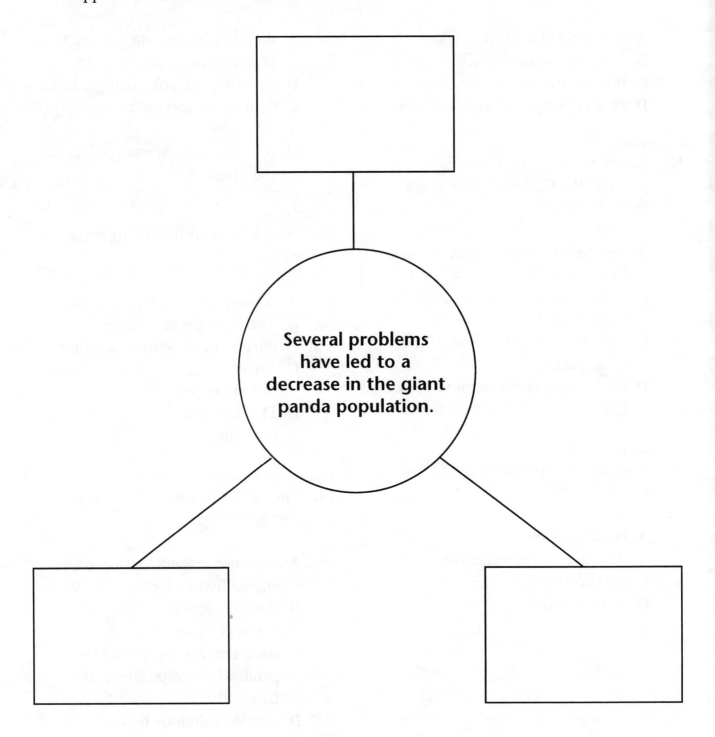

Several problems
have led to a
decrease in the giant
panda population.

58

7: The Bump

On a quiet, summer evening, Percy sat in his living room reading the newspaper, as he did every evening after dinner. The long, busy day was finally over, and he was ready for a rest.

As Percy reached for the sports section, he glanced at the small throw rug in front of the sofa. Was he seeing things? The rug had a bump in it. He looked again—the bump was moving. Percy rubbed his eyes and looked again. The bump wiggled **beneath** the rug!

Percy jumped up from his chair to put his hand on the bump, but his hand hit the solid floor. No bump! What was going on? Maybe the day had been longer and busier than he realized. He went to the kitchen to tell his wife, Leona, about his strange experience. Shaking her head in **disbelief**, she followed him back into the living room. No bump!

"You must have seen a shadow," she told him. Maybe, but he was sure about what he had seen. It seemed to quiver! Loosening his tie, Percy went back to his chair and newspaper, but now it was hard to concentrate on the news of the day. His eyes drifted back to the rug where the bump had first appeared. He saw nothing. Finally he gave up, returned to the newspaper, and settled into his reading.

After a few minutes, Percy heard it— a soft, low, sorrowful sound. He stopped reading and looked in the direction of the sound. It was coming from under the throw rug. The bump was back! But this time it was bigger and it moved from side to side. Percy grabbed his paper, rolled it into a club, and started for the bump. Raising the club high above his head, Percy swung hard and crashed it against the floor. There was a loud thud as his newspaper club hit the empty rug. Leona ran into the room.

"What are you doing?!"

"The bump came back and it was **quivering** and moaning," Percy explained.

"Your imagination is playing tricks on you," Leona scolded.

"Then where did the sound come from?"

"Maybe from a car outside, the wind in the trees...who knows? You were already upset, so you thought the sound came from the rug, too."

"You're probably right. It's been a long day. I think I'll go to bed. Good night." Percy slowly climbed the stairs and fell into a troubled sleep.

In no time, Percy was asleep, but he tossed and turned all night. Moaning and quivering bumps marched through all his dreams. When he woke the next morning, he was exhausted. He felt like he had not slept at all. Finally, Percy pulled himself up, shuffled to the bathroom, and stared at his face in the mirror.

"I look terrible!" he **murmured** to himself.

Percy took a long time getting dressed, but eventually he crept downstairs, dreading what he might see in the empty, darkened living room. He turned on the lights and opened the drapes. Slowly, he turned to look at the rug. Percy gave a sigh of relief.

"Thank goodness, that terrible bump is …"

Then, there it was! The bump under the rug was moving toward him!

Percy grabbed the nearest chair and smashed it solidly against the floor. He heard a low moan coming from under the rug. Again and again, Percy smashed the chair against the rug until he could no longer lift his arms. By the time he stopped, Percy had broken the chair into tiny pieces, knocked over the coffee table, and crashed a lamp to the floor. Panting and sweating, Percy dropped to the floor.

Leona had been watching from the doorway. "I'm glad that's over." Her whole body shook. "What do you suppose it was?"

"I don't even want to look," Percy replied. But they were both **drawn** to the spot. They inched forward, picked their way through the broken pieces of chair, and lifted the corner of the rug. They carefully and slowly pulled back the corner. **Nothing!**

"Do you think it went through the floor?" he wondered out loud.

"Maybe," Leona whispered, "but I don't want to go check."

Percy and Leona slowly cleaned up the pieces of broken chair and tried to forget the strange events. The next few days were almost normal. Percy read his evening paper at the kitchen table. Leona dusted and cleaned the house, but she stayed away from the living room.

After two weeks, Percy decided there was nothing to be afraid of, so he walked into the living room to look for a book. He switched on the light and began searching the bookshelf. Then he heard it—the soft, low, sorrowful moan from behind the couch. Percy didn't even turn around to look.

"Here we go again!"

Synonyms/Antonyms (I.D)

1. Which word means the OPPOSITE of **beneath**?

   A Below
   B Beside
   C Along
   D Above

Context Clues (I.B)

2. The word **quivering** means—

   A shaking
   B singing
   C crawling
   D moaning

Multiple Meanings (I.C)

3. In this passage, the word **drawn** means—

   A closed
   B sketched
   C attracted
   D poured

Context Clues (I.B)

4. The word **murmured** means—

   A screamed
   B jumped
   C mumbled
   D sang

Structural Cues (I.A)

5. In which word do the letters *dis* mean the same as in **disbelief**?

   A Dishwasher
   B Dishonesty
   C Distance
   D Childish

Sequential Order (II.B)

6. Which happened first in this passage?

   A The bump begins to quiver and moan.
   B Percy reads the newspaper in the kitchen.
   C Percy smashes a chair on the floor.
   D Leona tells Percy he has seen a shadow.

Setting (II.D)

7. Most of this passage happens—

   A at Percy's work place
   B in Leona and Percy's living room
   C in Leona and Percy's kitchen
   D under Leona and Percy's house

Inference (V.A)

8. Percy begins reading the newspaper at the kitchen table because—

A his wife asks him to read there
B the bump chases him away
C he is nervous about seeing the bump in the living room
D his wife is dusting and cleaning in the other room

Generalizations (V.C)

9. Which word best describes Percy's feelings when he sees the bump for the first time?

A Relieved
B Angry
C Startled
D Eager

Character Analysis (V.D)

10. How does Leona react when Percy first tells her about seeing the bump?

A She feels sorry for Percy because he is so tired.
B She is frightened and refuses to go in the living room.
C She ignores Percy and goes on working in the kitchen.
D She says Percy is imagining things.

Author's Purpose (VI.B)

11. The author probably wrote this passage to—

A persuade
B entertain
C inform
D describe

Identify Genres (VII.A)

12. Which type of writing is this passage?

A Adventure
B Mystery
C Folktale
D Legend

Literary Elements (VII.C)

13. Which word best describes the mood (general feeling) of this passage?

A Humorous
B Serious
C Gloomy
D Depressing

Summarize Ideas/Themes (III.B)

14. Write a brief summary of this passage for a friend who asks you what it is about.

Predictions (IV.B)

15. The passage ends with Percy saying, "Here we go again!" What do you think will happen next? Write what you think might happen next. Try to make the next events funny.

8: Selections by Sara Teasdale

April

by Sara Teasdale

The roofs are shining from the rain,
    The sparrows **twitter** as they fly,
And with a windy April grace
    The little clouds go by.

Yet the backyards are **bare** and brown
    With only one unchanging tree—
I could not be so sure of Spring
    Save that it sings in me.

The Cloud

by Sara Teasdale

I am a cloud in the heaven's height,
    The stars are lit for my delight,
Tireless and changeful, swift and free,
    I cast my shadow on hill and sea—
But why do the pines on the mountain's **crest**
    Call to me always, "Rest, rest"?

I throw my **mantle** over the moon
    And I blind the sun on his throne at noon,
Nothing can tame me, nothing can bind,
    I am a child of the **heartless** wind—
But oh the pines on the mountain's crest
    Whispering always, "Rest, rest."

Context Clues (I.B)
1. What does the word **twitter** mean?

   A Create
   B Fall
   C Chirp
   D Gnaw

Synonyms/Antonyms (I.D)
2. Which word means about the same as **bare** in "April"?

   A Leafy
   B Empty
   C Broken
   D Rocky

Multiple Meanings (I.C)
3. In "The Cloud," the word **crest** means a—

   A peak
   B bird's head
   C shield
   D wave

Context Clues (I.B)
4. In "The Cloud," the word **mantle** means the cloud's—

   A shadow
   B color
   C delight
   D throne

Structural Cues (I.A)
5. In which word do the letters *less* mean the same as in **heartless**?

   A Lesson
   B Blessing
   C Fearless
   D Lessen

Facts/Details (II.A)
6. In "The Cloud," what tells the cloud to rest?

   A Its shadow
   B The stars
   C The sun
   D The pine trees

Summarize Ideas/Themes (III.B)
7. Which of the following would be another good title for "April"?

   A Birds in the Sky
   B Windy April
   C Waiting for Spring
   D Trees

Cause/Effect (IV.A)
8. In "The Cloud," the sun is blinded because the—

   A moon and stars are in the sky
   B wind blows so hard
   C cloud covers it
   D pines whisper on the mountain

Figurative Language (VII.D)

9. In "The Cloud," a cloud is the speaker. This is an example of—

  A a simile
  B alliteration
  C rhythm
  D personification

Figurative Language (VII.D)

10. In "April," the author repeats the **b** sound in this line: "Yet the backyards are bare and brown." This is an example of—

  A a metaphor
  B alliteration
  C rhyme
  D a simile

Identify Genre (VII.A)

11. "April" and "The Cloud" are both—

  A narratives
  B paragraphs
  C poems
  D essays

Generalizations (V.C)

12. Which word best describes how the writer feels at the end of "April"?

  A Depressed
  B Frightened
  C Heartless
  D Hopeful

Similarities/Differences (IV.C)

13. Write two paragraphs about "April" and "The Cloud." In the first paragraph, explain how the two passages are alike. In the second paragraph, explain how the two passages are different. Use information from each passage in your answer.

9: Butterflies On the Go

Many birds **migrate** south when it is cold in the northern areas of the country. Did you know that some butterflies also travel to warmer places? Every year, monarch butterflies go on an **unusual** journey as they travel from the north to the south, and then back to the north again.

The monarchs begin from two areas in the United States. Some of the butterflies live west of the Rocky Mountains. They migrate to the **southern** coast of California each fall. Other butterflies live east of the Rocky Mountains. They migrate to the plains of Mexico each year.

How can such small creatures travel so far? Scientists really aren't sure how they do it. The monarch butterflies may use wind **currents** to carry them far away. The high winds from storms could carry them for many, many miles. They also may have a special system for sensing direction. By using it, they always know which way they are going.

The monarchs that begin each trip do not return to the north in the spring. They don't live long enough to complete such a long trip. The butterflies that begin the trip lay eggs during their **journey**. The caterpillars that hatch from these eggs eventually spin cocoons. Young butterflies **emerge** from the cocoons and continue the journey their parents began. The young butterflies return to the same trees

other monarchs have used for years. How do they find a place they have never seen? No one knows just how they do it—but they do it every year.

Monarch butterflies complete a trip that few people could make. They are amazing creatures!

Context Clues (I.B)

1. The word **migrate** means—

    A fly high in the clouds
    B rest in the trees
    C begin a difficult trip
    D move from one climate to another

Structural Cues (I.A)

2. In which word do the letters *ern* mean the same as in **southern**?

    A Govern
    B Stern
    C Western
    D Fern

Context Clues (I.B)

3. In this passage, the word **currents** means—

A storms

B disasters

C movements

D systems

Synonyms/Antonyms (I.D)

4. Which word means about the same as **journey**?

A Trip

B Hatch

C Direction

D Spring

Synonyms/Antonyms (I.D)

5. Which word means the OPPOSITE of **unusual**?

A Odd

B Normal

C Strange

D Dangerous

Context Clues (I.B)

6. The word **emerge** means—

A follow

B fall

C come from

D spin

Facts/Details (II.A)

7. Monarch butterflies west of the Rocky Mountains migrate—

A in different directions

B to the east of the Rocky Mountains

C to Mexico

D to the southern coast of California

Main Idea (III.A)

8. This passage is mostly about—

A how monarch butterflies locate wind currents

B why caterpillars spin cocoons

C the movement of monarch butterflies from one place to another

D how scientists have learned about monarch butterflies

Cause/Effect (IV.A)

9. The monarch butterflies that begin the journey do not finish because they—

A return to their home after laying eggs

B do not live long enough to finish

C cannot find the right wind currents

D do not always know where they are going

70

Sequential Order (II.B)

10. Which of the following happens first?

A Caterpillars hatch from the eggs.
B Caterpillars spin cocoons.
C Monarch butterflies emerge from cocoons.
D Monarch butterflies lay eggs.

Inferences (V.A)

11. Monarch butterflies migrate south when it is cold in the north because they—

A cannot survive in cold weather
B must lay their eggs somewhere
C use the wind currents
D must return to the same trees each year

Fact/Opinion (VI.A)

12. Which is an OPINION from this passage?

A Monarch butterflies live in the United States.
B Young monarch butterflies emerge from cocoons.
C Monarch butterflies are truly amazing creatures.
D Caterpillars spin cocoons.

Facts/Details (II.A)

13. Complete the diagram below by listing facts and details from the passage that support the main idea written in the circle.

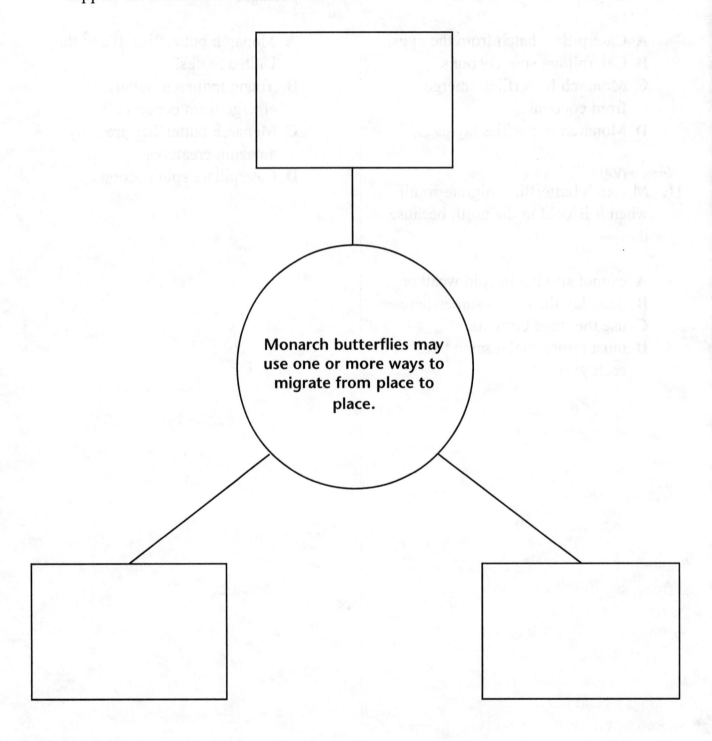

Monarch butterflies may use one or more ways to migrate from place to place.

10: Rebecca of Sunnybrook Farm

The following passage is from the first chapter of Rebecca of Sunnybrook Farm, *a book by Kate Douglas Wiggin.*

 The old stagecoach rumbled along the dusty road that runs from Maplewood to Riverboro. The day was warm as midsummer, though it was only the middle of May. Mr. Jeremiah Cobb favored the horses as much as possible, yet never forgot that he carried the mail. The reins lay loosely in his hands as he stretched back in his seat. He **extended** one foot and leg over the dashboard. His brimmed old felt hat was pulled over his eyes.

There was one passenger in the coach—a small, dark-haired girl in a glossy calico dress. She was so slender and so stiffly starched that she slid from space to space on the leather cushions. To keep some sort of balance, the girl braced herself against the middle seat with her feet and extended her cotton-gloved hands on each side. Whenever the wheels sank farther than usual into a rut or jolted suddenly over a stone, she bounced into the air and came down again. Then she pushed back her funny little straw hat and firmly held a small, pink sun shade, which seemed to be her main responsibility. The girl also had a bead purse, into which she looked whenever the condition of the roads would permit. She was always happy to see that the purse's contents had not disappeared.

Mr. Cobb knew nothing of these bothersome details of travel. His business was to carry people to their **destination**, not to make them comfortable on the way. Indeed, he had forgotten about his one little passenger.

When he was about to leave the post office in Maplewood earlier that morning, a woman climbed down from a wagon. Coming up to him, she asked whether this was the Riverboro stage and if he were Mr. Cobb. When he answered yes to both questions, she nodded to a child who was eagerly waiting for the answer. As if she feared being a moment too late, the child ran toward the woman. Her mother helped her into the stagecoach and placed a bundle and a bouquet of lilacs beside her. Then the woman watched as an old **trunk** was roped on to the coach. Finally the woman paid the fare, counting out the silver coins with great care.

"I want you to take her to my sisters in Riverboro," she said. "Do you know Mirandy and Jane Sawyer? They live in a brick house."

Mr. Cobb told her that he knew them well.

"Well, she's going there. They're expecting her. Will you keep an eye on her, please? If she can get out anywhere and get with folks, or get anybody in to keep her company, she'll do it."

Then the woman turned toward the girl. "Good-bye, Rebecca. Try not to get into any mischief. Sit quietly so you'll look neat and nice when you get there. Don't be any trouble to Mr. Cobb."

"Good-bye, Mother. Don't worry. You know it isn't as if I haven't traveled before."

The woman gave a short laugh and explained to Mr. Cobb, "She's been to Wareham and stayed over night. That isn't much to be journey-proud on!"

"It was traveling, Mother," said the child. "It was leaving the farm. We put lunch in a basket and did a little riding and went on little steam cars. And we carried our night gowns."

"Don't tell the whole village about it, if we did," said the mother, interrupting her daughter. "Haven't I told you before?" she whispered. "You shouldn't talk about night gowns and stockings and things like that in a loud tone of voice."

"I know, Mother, I know. All I want to say is..." Mr. Cobb gave a cluck, slapped the reins, and the horses started on their daily task.

"...all I want to say is that it is a journey when..." The stage was really under way now, and Rebecca had to put her head out of the window and over the door in order to finish her sentence.

"It is a journey when you carry a night gown!"

The **objectionable** word floated back to Mrs. Randall's offended ears. She watched the stage out of sight. Then she gathered up her packages from the bench at the store and stepped into the wagon that had been standing at the hitching post. As she turned the horse's head toward home, she rose to her feet for a moment. Shading her eyes with her hand, she looked at a cloud of dust in the **dim** distance.

"Mirandy will have her hands full, I guess," she said to herself, "but I wouldn't be surprised if it would be the making of Rebecca."

Synonyms/Antonyms (I.D)

1. Which word means about the same as **extended**?

A Stood
B Stretched
C Covered
D Carried

Context Clues (I.B)

2. What does the word **destination** mean?

A Travel
B Journey's end
C Comfort
D Passenger

Context Clues (I.B)

3. The word **dim** means—

A bright
B large
C faraway
D unclear

Structural Cues (I.A)

4. In which word do the letters *able* mean the same as in the word **objectionable**?

A Tablecloth
B Cable
C Forgettable
D Tablet

Multiple Meanings (I.C)

5. In this passage, the word **trunk** means—

A the main stem of a tree
B an elephant's nose
C a piece of luggage
D a part of a river

Facts/Details (II.A)

6. Who is Rebecca's mother?

A Mrs. Randall
B Jane Sawyer
C Mirandy Sawyer
D Mrs. Cobb

Sequential Order (II.B)

7. When does Rebecca's mother ask Mr. Cobb if he knows her sisters?

A Before Rebecca gets on the stagecoach
B As soon as she meets him
C After paying Rebecca's fare
D After the stagecoach begins to leave

Setting (II.D)

8. This story probably takes place—

A in modern times
B 50 years from now
C in 1950
D around 1900

Main Idea (III.A)
9. This passage is mostly about—

A a young girl's leaving to visit her aunts
B how people travel on stagecoaches
C how a young girl gets ready for a trip on a stagecoach
D why a young girl is going to visit her aunts

Cause/Effect (IV.A)
10. Rebecca's mother begins to whisper because she—

A wants to tell Mr. Cobb a secret
B is tired and ready for Rebecca to leave
C wants Rebecca to lower her voice
D is counting out the coins for Rebecca's fare

Predictions (IV.B)
11. How will Rebecca probably feel during the trip to her aunts' house?

A Frightened
B Excited
C Nervous
D Jealous

Inferences (V.A)
12. Rebecca's mother thinks Mirandy will have her hands full because—

A Rebecca has too much luggage
B Mirandy does not know Rebecca is coming
C the stagecoach probably will arrive late
D Rebecca may not behave in the right way

Character Analysis (V.D)
13. When Rebecca's mother talks to Mr. Cobb about Rebecca and the trip, she seems to be—

A angry
B relieved
C worried
D forgetful

Character Analysis (V.D)

14. What kind of child does Rebecca seem to be? For example, is she naughty? Is she polite and well-mannered? How do you know? In the center circle, write one or two words to describe her. Then find information from the passage to support your description. Write that information in the boxes around the circle.

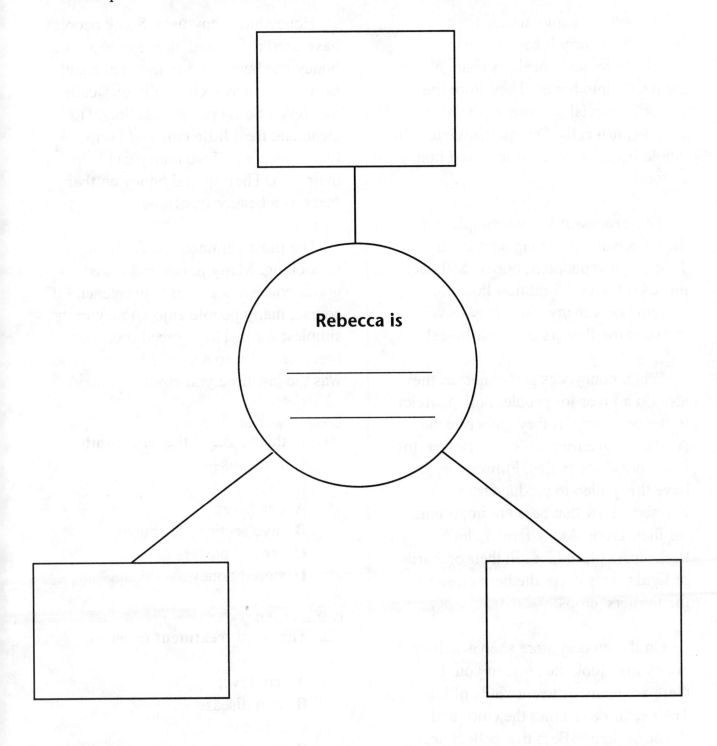

11: A Taste of Honey

Honey is the oldest sweetener on earth. It is a sweet treat for many people, but it is food for the honeybees. The bees must have honey to survive.

Honeybees gather nectar from flowers and carry it back to their hives. There the honeybees change the nectar into honey. They store the nectar in special sections of the hive called **comb cells**. During the winter, the whole bee colony uses the stored honey as food.

The **process** may look simple, but the bees work hard to make their honey. To make one pound of honey, 550 bees must visit over 2.5 million flowers. Imagine how many miles they travel between the flowers and their hives!

When honeybees gather nectar, they also do a favor for people. Pollen **sticks** to the bees' legs as they gather nectar. As they move from flower to flower, the bees spread the pollen. Flowers must have this pollen to produce fruit. Farmers know that bees are important for their crops. Many farmers let beekeepers place hives in their orchards or fields. This keeps the bees close to the farmers' crops.

On the grocery store shelves, all honey may look the same to you, but there are many different kinds of honey. The nectar determines the color and flavor of honey. Bees that collect nectar from raspberry plants produce raspberry honey which is light and clear. Other bees may gather nectar from buckwheat plants. Buckwheat honey is dark and has a strong taste.

Honey has many uses. Some people have used it for medicine. For example, honey has been used to treat bone and skin diseases as well as allergies called hay fever. Some people use honey to clean and treat little cuts and burns. Other people believe honey can help their skin. They spread honey on their faces as a beauty **treatment**.

The most common use for honey is in cooking. Many jellies and baked goods contain honey as a sweetener. Of course, many people enjoy honey in its simplest form. They spread it on warm bread or add it to a cup of hot tea. When was the last time you enjoyed honey?

Context Clues (I.B)

1. In this passage, the term **comb cells** means—

   A bee hives
   B hive sections for honey
   C special powers
   D stored honey

Context Clues (I.B)

2. The word **treatment** means—

   A hay fever
   B skin disease
   C skin care
   D cut

Synonyms/Antonyms (I.D)

3. Which word means about the same as the word **process**?

A Travel
B Pound
C Hive
D Method

Multiple Meanings (I.C)

4. In this passage, the word **sticks** means—

A small pieces of wood
B attaches
C pokes
D lasts

Facts/Details (II.A)

5. According to the passage, what is the most common use for honey?

A As a medicine
B As a skin treatment
C In cooking
D As a cleaner

Main Idea (III.A)

6. The **second** paragraph is mostly about—

A why people like honey
B the special power of honey
C why honey is special
D how bees make and store honey

Cause/Effect (IV.A)

7. Each kind of honey has a special flavor and color because—

A each kind of honey is made from different nectar
B each kind of honey has a different use
C each kind of honey is made by different bees
D some people like honey that has a strong taste

Inferences (V.A)

8. Honey is often used in food because—

A most recipes need honey
B it is the only sweetener people have
C food with honey is good for people
D it adds a sweet taste to food

Generalizations (V.C)

9. You can tell from the passage that—

A honey is one of the best medicines for people
B bees must work to make the food they need
C honey is the best sweetener for tea
D raspberry honey tastes better than buckwheat honey

Fact/Opinion (VI.A)

10. Which is a FACT in the passage?

    A All kinds of honey taste and look the same.

    B Some people use honey on cuts and burns.

    C Buckwheat honey is too dark and too strong to eat.

    D Everyone should eat honey.

Summarize Ideas/Themes (III.B)

11. Write a three- to four-sentence summary of this passage. Use information from the passage in your answer.

12: Pandora's Box

A myth is a story that people tell to explain why something happens in life. Pandora is a famous character from the Greek myths. Gods and goddesses are in many Greek myths.

*In the myth about Pandora, the gods try to make the perfect woman. The woman is not a goddess, but the gods give her many **traits** of the gods. This myth connects Pandora's mistakes to the bad things that happen in the world.*

Zeus and Hephestus, two Greek gods, decided to make a perfect woman. Each god and goddess gave something to make her special. Aphrodite gave her fresh beauty like spring. Athena dressed the woman and placed **garlands** of flowers around her neck. Hermes gave her curiosity and the ability to trick people. The woman needed a special name because all the gods had given her special gifts. They named their perfect woman Pandora. This special name means "gifted by all the gods."

The gods gave Pandora one last gift. It was a wooden chest. They told her that it held a great treasure. They also said that Pandora should never open the box.

Zeus offered Pandora to the god Epimetheus as a gift. Epimetheus didn't know if he should take the gift. His brother warned him never to take a gift from Zeus. However, Epimetheus took Pandora. He thought she had great beauty and charm. For a while, Pandora and Epimetheus lived together in happiness.

Day after day, Pandora grew more curious about the box. After a while, her curiosity got the best of her. She wanted to see the gifts in the lovely chest.

One day Pandora was alone. She went to the corner where the box lay. She carefully lifted the lid for a quick **peek** inside. To her surprise, the lid flew open and out of her hand. Pandora fell away from the box. Strange **shadowy** shapes flew wildly from the box. They flew in all directions. The stream of figures seemed never to end. The shapes were all the bad things in the world. Hunger, disease, jealousy, war, greed, anger, and fear escaped from the box.

At first, Pandora couldn't move. When she could finally get up, she quickly shut the box lid. She thought it was too late. She thought all the evil had escaped, but Pandora had kept one special thing. She had saved the gift of hope.

Ever since that time, hope has helped people through hard times and troubles. They can live with the sorrows that escaped from Pandora's box because they have hope. Pandora **disobeyed** the orders from the gods, but she saved the most important thing of all—hope.

Context Clues (I.B)

1. What does the word **traits** mean?

A Qualities
B Flowers
C Stories
D Mistakes

Context Clues (I.B)

2. In this passage, the word **garlands** means—

A chests
B figures
C necklaces
D surprises

Structural Cues (I.A)

3. In which word do the letters *dis* mean the same as in the word **disobeyed**?

A Dish
B Childish
C Disappear
D Diskette

Synonyms/Antonyms (I.D)

4. Which word means about the same as the word **peek**?

A Cover
B Look
C Surprise
D Gift

Structural Cues (I.A)

5. What does the word **shadowy** mean?

A Light
B Deep
C Wild
D Unclear

Facts/Details (II.A)

6. Which god receives Pandora as a gift?

A Zeus
B Hephestus
C Hermes
D Epimetheus

Sequential Order (II.B)

7. What happens right after Pandora lifts the box lid?

A Shadowy shapes fly in all directions.
B The lid flies open and out of her hand.
C Pandora receives gifts from the gods and goddesses.
D Pandora saves hope.

Main Idea (III.A)

8. This Greek myth is mostly about—

A the power of the gods to change lives
B how Pandora and Epimetheus live in happiness
C a character whose curiosity causes problems in the world
D why the Greeks had myths

Cause/Effect (IV.A)
9. Pandora lifts the lid of the box because she—

   A wants the shadowy figures to escape
   B wants to see what is inside
   C thinks Epimetheus will be happy
   D knows it holds the best gifts

Inferences (V.A)
10. Pandora tries to shut the box quickly in order to—

   A stop more evil from escaping
   B hide her mistake from Epimetheus
   C show that she is strong
   D keep all the evil in the box

Fact/Opinion (VI.A)
11. Which is a FACT from the passage?

   A Aphrodite gives flowers to Pandora.
   B Hermes takes Pandora to Epimetheus.
   C Epimetheus distrusts Zeus.
   D Pandora is more beautiful than Athena.

Identify Genres (VII.A)
12. Which of the following type of writing is a myth?

   A Biography
   B Nonfiction
   C Poetry
   D Fiction

Literary Elements (VII.C)
13. Which event in the story causes the greatest problem in "Pandora's Box"?

   A Aphrodite gives Pandora the gift of beauty.
   B Pandora disobeys the gods' orders.
   C Pandora goes to live with Epimetheus.
   D Zeus and Hephestus decide to make the perfect woman.

Figurative Language (VII.D)
14. Aphrodite gives Pandora "fresh beauty like spring." *Fresh beauty like spring* is an example of—

   A a metaphor
   B rhyme
   C alliteration
   D a simile

Predictions (IV.B)

15. What might happen when the gods learn that Pandora opened the chest? Predict what you think will happen. Give reasons for your prediction.

_____

_____

_____

_____

_____

_____

_____

_____

_____

_____

_____

13: The River Bank

The following passage is adapted from The Wind in the Willows *by Kenneth Grahame. It is springtime, and the Water Rat has taken his friend Mole on his very first boat ride.*

Leaving the main stream, they now passed into what seemed at first sight like a little land-locked lake. Green turf sloped down to either edge, and brown snaky tree roots gleamed below the surface of the quiet water. Ahead of them, the silvery shoulder and foamy tumble of a dam filled the air with a soothing murmur of sound. It was so very beautiful that the Mole could only hold up both forepaws and gasp, "Oh my! Oh my! Oh my!"

The Rat brought the boat alongside the bank and made her fast. Then he helped the still **awkward** Mole safely ashore and swung out the luncheon basket. Mole begged to unpack it all by himself, and the Rat was very pleased to allow him. The Rat sprawled at full length on the grass and rested while his excited friend shook out the tablecloth and spread it. Mole took out all the mysterious packets one by one and arranged their contents in due order, still gasping, "Oh my! Oh my!" at each new one. When all was ready, the Rat said, "Now, pitch in, old fellow!" Mole was indeed very glad to obey. He had started his spring cleaning at a very early hour that morning and had not paused for bite or drink. He had been through a very

great deal since that distant time, which now seemed so many days ago.

"What are you looking at?" said the Rat presently, when the edge of their hunger was somewhat dulled, and the Mole's eyes were able to wander off the tablecloth a little.

"I am looking," said the Mole, "at a streak of bubbles that are traveling along the surface of the water. That is a thing that strikes me as funny."

"Bubbles? Oh!" said the Rat, and **chirruped** cheerily in an inviting sort of way.

A broad glistening **muzzle** showed itself above the edge of the bank, and the Otter hauled himself out and shook the water from his coat.

"Greedy beggars!" he observed, making for the food. "Why didn't you invite me, Ratty?"

"This was an impromptu *(unplanned)* affair," explained the Rat. "By the way—my friend Mr. Mole."

"Proud, I'm sure," said the Otter, and the two animals were friends immediately.

"Such a **rumpus** everywhere!" continued the Otter. "All the world seems out on the river today. I came up this backwater to get a moment's peace, and then stumble upon you fellows! At least—I beg pardon—I don't exactly mean that, you know."

There was a rustle behind them. It came from a hedge where last year's leaves still clung thick. Soon a striped head, with high shoulders behind it, peered forth on them.

"Come on, old Badger!" shouted the Rat.

The Badger trotted forward a pace or two, then grunted, "H'm! Company!" and turned his back and disappeared from view.

"That's *just* the sort of fellow he is!" observed the disappointed Rat. "Simply hates Society! Now we won't see any more of him today. Well, tell us, who's out on the river?"

"Toad's out, for one," replied the Otter. "In his brand new row boat; new clothes, new everything!"

The two animals looked at each other and laughed.

"Once, it was nothing but sailing," said the Rat. "Then he tired of that and took to punting.* Nothing would please him but to punt all day and every day. Last year it was houseboating. We all had to go and stay with him in his houseboat and pretend we liked it. He was going to spend the rest of his life in a houseboat. It's all the same, whatever he takes up. He gets tired of it and starts on something fresh."

"Such a good fellow, too," remarked the Otter, "but no **stability**—especially in a boat!"

From where they sat, they could glimpse the main stream across the island that separated them. Just then a boat flashed into view, the rower—a short, stout figure—splashing badly and rolling a good deal, but working his hardest. The Rat stood up and hailed him, but Toad—for it was he—shook his head and settled sternly to his work.

"He'll be out of the boat in a minute if he rolls like that," said the Rat, sitting down again.

"Of course he will," chuckled the Otter. "Did I ever tell you that good story about Toad and the lockkeeper? It happened this way. Toad ..."

* *A punt is a long, flat-bottomed boat. A punter moves the boat through the water with a long pole.*

Multiple Meanings (I.C)
1. What does the word **muzzle** mean in this passage?

   A Part of a gun
   B To stop someone from speaking
   C An animal's nose
   D A covering for a dog's mouth

Context Clues (I.B)
2. The word **rumpus** means—

   A wrinkles
   B a wet area
   C a noisy situation
   D a picnic

Synonyms/Antonyms (I.D)
3. Which word means about the same as **awkward**?

   A Scared
   B Clumsy
   C Silly
   D Strange

Context Clues (I.B)
4. The word **stability** means—

   A kindness
   B sail boat
   C stream
   D firmness

Context Clues (I.B)
5. The word **chirruped** means—

   A growled
   B chirped
   C traveled
   D bubbled

Sequential Order (II.B)
6. When do Mole and Rat first see Toad in his new boat?

   A Just before they eat their lunch
   B Just before Otter visits them
   C After Otter leaves them
   D After Otter tells them he has seen Toad

Setting (II.D)
7. Most of the events in this story take place—

   A on the banks of a stream
   B at Rat's home
   C on Toad's new boat
   D near Mole's home

Cause/Effect (IV.A)
8. Badger does not stay to eat with Rat and Mole because—

   A they do not have enough food for him
   B he does not like to be with others
   C he does not like the food they are eating
   D Otter asks him to leave them alone

87

Predictions (IV.B)

9. At the end of this part of the story, Otter is probably going to—

A ask Rat to follow after Toad

B look for Badger

C tell what happened between Toad and the lockkeeper

D talk about Toad's new boat

Inferences (V.A)

10. Rat and Otter laugh when Otter tells about Toad's new boat because they—

A wish they had the same kind of boat

B want Badger to come back and join them

C know Toad always changes his mind about what kind of boat is best

D think Toad looks strange in his new clothes

Character Analysis (V.D)

11. Which word best describes Mole's feelings when he sees the stream and the dam?

A Scared

B Jealous

C Disappointed

D Excited

Inferences (V.A)

12. Mole keeps saying, "Oh my! Oh my!" because he—

A worries about falling in the water

B likes the things he is seeing and doing for the first time

C feels sick from the boat ride

D wants to return to his home

Figurative Language (VII.D)

13. In this passage, Rat, Mole, Otter, and Badger can talk. This is an example of—

A exaggeration

B personification

C literature

D metaphor

88

Similarities/Differences (IV.C)

14. Choose two characters from this story. How are these two characters the same? How are they different? Record your ideas on the Venn diagram below.

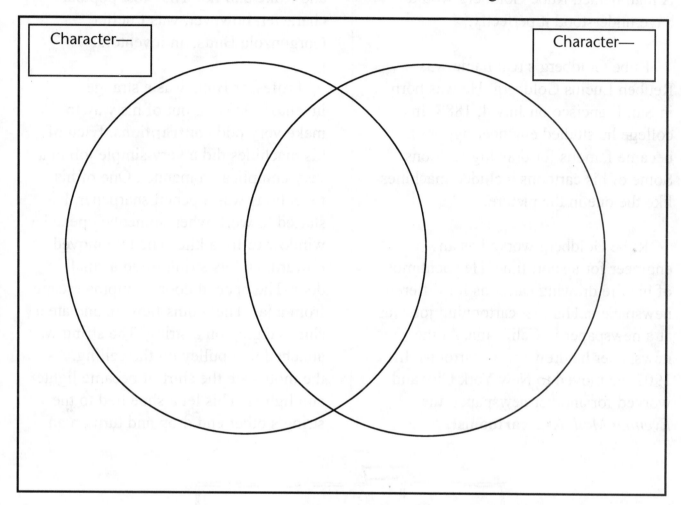

Character—

Character—

14: How Do You Sharpen a Pencil?

That's quite a machine at the bottom of the page, isn't it? How does it work? A man named Rube Goldberg would have understood it perfectly.

Rube Goldberg's real name was Reuben Lucius Goldberg. He was born in San Francisco on July 4, 1883. In college he studied engineering, but he became famous for drawing cartoons. Some of his cartoons included machines like the one in the picture.

Rube Goldberg worked as an engineer for a short time. He spent most of his life drawing cartoons for different newspapers. His first cartooning job was at a newspaper in California. At the newspaper he drew sports cartoons. In 1907, he moved to New York City and worked for another newspaper, the *Evening Mail*. As a **cartoonist**,

Goldberg created many cartoon characters: Boob McNutt, Lala Palooza, and Mike and Ike. His most popular character, however, was Lucifer Gorgonzola Butts, an inventor.

Professor Butts was a strange inventor. He went out of his way to make very odd **contraptions**. Each of his machines did a very simple job in a very complicated manner. One of his inventions was a pencil sharpener. It started to work when someone opened a window to fly a kite. The kite moved upward, and its string lifted a small door. The opened door let moths escape from a jar. The moths flew up and ate a shirt hanging on a string. The string was attached to a pulley on the ceiling. As the moths ate the shirt, it became lighter and lighter. This let a shoe tied to the string's other end drop and turn on an

CANDLE BURNS STRING (A) DROPPING ROCK (B) ON LEVER (C) WHICH PUSHES UP ROD (D) TRIPPING LEVER (E) DROPPING GLASS OF WATER (F) INTO LEAKING BUCKET (G) TURNING TURBINE (H) WHICH DRIVES CLOCK WORKS.

electric iron. The iron overheated and burned a hole in a pair of **trousers**. The smoke from the pants floated out the window and entered a hole in a nearby tree. The smoke caused an opossum to leave the tree. The opossum jumped into a basket attached to another string. When the basket dropped, its string lifted a cage that covered a woodpecker. The woodpecker escaped and pecked on the end of a nearby pencil. The bird's pecking exposed the pencil's lead. So, at last, the pencil was sharp!

Of course, there are much easier ways to sharpen a pencil. Why did Rube Goldberg make it so hard? His cartoon was a **satire** about modern technology. A satire is a work that uses humor to show how foolish or evil some accepted idea or practice may be. In his cartoons, Goldberg made fun of modern technology. He thought modern machines sometimes made life harder, even though they were supposed to make life easier.

Rube Goldberg was one of the most famous cartoonists of all time. People loved his cartoons about the inventions of Professor Butts. In fact, "Rube Goldberg" is now an entry in many dictionaries. It is defined as a machine that does a simple job in a complex and indirect way.

In 1948, Rube Goldberg won a Pulitzer Prize for his cartoons. He retired as a cartoonist in 1964. He

continued his creative work. After retirement, he earned recognition for his bronze and clay sculptures. He died on December 7, 1970, but his cartoons still make us smile today.

Structural Cues (I.A)
1. In which word do the letters *ist* mean the same as in **cartoonist**?

   A Mister
   B Listing
   C Fist
   D Pianist

Context Clues (I.B)
2. The word **contraptions** means—

   A cartoons
   B characters
   C newspapers
   D machines

Synonyms/Antonyms (I.D)
3. Which word means about the same as **trousers**?

   A Baskets
   B Pants
   C Clothes
   D Kites

Context Clues (I.B)

4. The word **satire** means a—

A funny cartoon

B complicated modern machine

C work that uses humor to show how foolish an idea is

D cartoon created by Rube Goldberg

Facts/Details (II.A)

5. Rube Goldberg's most popular character, Professor Lucifer Gornonzola Butts, was a(n)—

A engineer

B cartoonist

C newspaper reporter

D inventor

Sequential Order (II.B)

6. In Professor Butts' pencil sharpener, what happened just before the basket dropped?

A The opposum jumped into the basket.

B Smoke entered the opposum's tree.

C The woodpecker escaped from its cage.

D The kite's string opened the small door.

Follow Directions (II.C)

7. Look at the diagram on page 90. What happens right after the candle burns the string?

A The rock drops.

B The lever pushes the rod.

C The glass of water drops.

D The bucket leaks.

Summarize Ideas/Themes (III.B)

8. Which is the best summary of this passage?

A Rube Goldberg worked as a cartoonist at several newspapers.

B People enjoyed the cartoons created by Rube Goldberg because the cartoons were funny.

C The famous cartoonist Rube Goldberg entertained people with cartoons that poked fun at modern machines.

D Modern machines sometimes make life more complicated and difficult.

Cause/Effect (IV.A)

9. Rube Goldberg made fun of modern machines because he—

A did not understand how they worked

B believed they sometimes made life harder instead of easier

C wanted his name to be in the dictionary

D wanted to be an engineer instead of a cartoonist

Inferences (V.A)

10. People probably loved Rube Goldberg's cartoons because they—

A hated all modern machines
B loved all newspaper cartoons
C did not know how machines worked
D agreed with some of his ideas about modern machines

Generalizations (V.C)

11. You can tell that Rube Goldberg's cartoons probably—

A would not be funny to people today
B were too complicated for most people to understand
C took a lot of time and effort from Goldberg
D were funnier than any other cartoons in the newspaper

Generalizations (V.C)

12. Which of the following best describes Rube Goldberg?

A Foolish
B Unsuccessful
C Creative
D Difficult

Fact/Opinion (VI.A)

13. Which is a FACT from this passage?

A Modern machines make everyone's life more difficult.
B Rube Goldberg should have been an engineer.
C Rube Goldberg also made bronze and clay sculptures.
D Rube Goldberg's cartoons were more popular than the cartoons created by other people.

Identify Genres (VII.A); Genre Characteristics (VII.B)

14. Is this passage fiction or nonfiction? How do you know? Use information from the passage in your answer.

15: Mr. Nobody

I know a funny little man,
    As quiet as a mouse,
Who does the mischief that is done
    In everybody's house!
Now no one ever sees his face,
    And yet we all agree
That every **plate** we break was cracked
    By Mr. Nobody.

It's he who always tears our books,
    Who leaves the door **ajar**,
He pulls the buttons from our shirts,
    And **scatters** pins afar;
That squeaking door will always squeak
    For, my goodness, don't you see,
We leave the oiling to be done
    By Mr. Nobody.

He puts damp wood upon the fire,
    So that kettles cannot boil;
His are the feet that bring in mud,
    And all the carpets soil.
The papers always are **mislaid**,
    Who has them last but he?
There's not one tosses them about
    But Mr. Nobody.

The finger **smudges** on the door
    By none of us are made;
We never leave the blinds unclosed,
    To let the curtains fade;
The milk will never spill; the boots
    That lying around you see
Are not our boots; they all belong
    To Mr. Nobody.

—*Author Unknown*

©ECS Learning Systems, Inc.

1. What does the word **ajar** mean?

   A Closed tightly
   B Alone
   C Slightly open
   D Ripped

Synonyms/Antonyms (I.D)
2. Which word means about the same as **scatters**?

   A Spreads
   B Gathers
   C Picks
   D Pulls

Structural Cues (I.A)
3. In which word do the letters *mis* mean the same as in **mislaid**?

   A Misery
   B Missing
   C Promise
   D Mishandle

Context Clues (I.B)
4. The word **smudges** means—

   A doors
   B stains
   C walls
   D spills

Multiple Meanings (I.C)

5. In this passage, the word **plate** means—

   A pane
   B base
   C layer
   D dish

Facts/Details (II.A)

6. What does Mr. Nobody do with the buttons on shirts?

   A Leaves them in the doorway
   B Pulls them off
   C Spills them on the floor
   D Scatters them around

Cause/Effect (IV.A)

7. In this passage, the kettles cannot boil because Mr. Nobody—

   A leaves the door open
   B loses the wood for the fire
   C puts damp wood on the fire
   D spills water on the floor

Inferences (V.A)

8. The author of this passage blames Mr. Nobody for everything that goes wrong in everybody's house because—

   A the author saw him do these things
   B no one else will admit to doing these things
   C Mr. Nobody told the author about doing these things
   D the author wants people to be more careful around Mr. Nobody

Author's Purpose (VI.B)

9. The author probably wrote this passage to—

   A entertain readers
   B explain why things go wrong in everybody's house
   C persuade readers to be helpful
   D explain what needs to be done in everybody's house

Literary Elements (VII.C)

10. Tone is the general feeling of a passage. What is the tone of this passage?

    A Serious
    B Gloomy
    C Humorous
    D Mysterious

Figurative Language (VII.D)

11. The passage states that the funny little man is *as quiet as a mouse.*
As quiet as a mouse is an example of—

A rhyme
B alliteration
C exaggeration
D a simile

Identify Genres (VII.A); Genre Characteristics (VII.B)

12. Is this passage fiction, nonfiction, or poetry? How do you know? Use information from the passage in your answer.

Notes

Study Skills

VIII. **Identify and use sources of different types of information**

    A. Use and interpret graphic sources of information

    B. Use reference resources and the parts of a book to locate information

    C. Recognize and use dictionary skills

99

Notes

Practice 1: Study Skills

Directions: Read each question. Then choose the best answer. On your answer sheet, darken the circle for the correct answer.

This is part of an index from a geography book. Use it to answer the questions.

Canada, 315–333
   borders of, 315–316
   climate of, 317–319
   farming in, 326–329
   fishing in, 330
   government of, 331–333
   landforms of, 320–322
   natural resources in, 323–325

China, 227–239
   climate of, 227–230
   culture of, 237–239
   farming in, 234–236
   landforms of, 231–233

Cities, 185–201
   earliest cities of world, 187–188
   employment in, 194–195
   growth of, 189–193
   history of, 185–187
   pollution in, 200–201
   services in, 196–199

---

1. This book does not include information about China's—

   A climate
   B landforms
   C farming
   D natural resources

2. On which page could you begin reading about the government of Canada?

   A 315
   B 320
   C 331
   D 333

3. To find out about jobs available in a city, you would begin reading on page—

   A 185
   B 189
   C 194
   D 201

4. To find out which crops are grown in China, you would begin reading on page—

   A 234
   B 236
   C 315
   D 326

5. On which pages could you look to read about the very first cities?

   A 185–201
   B 187–188
   C 194–195
   D 196–199

Practice 2: Study Skills

Directions: Read each question. Then choose the best answer. On your answer sheet, darken the circle for the correct answer.

This is part of the table of contents from a book called *Ideas in Science*. Use it to answer the questions.

1. Which information would probably be found in Chapter Five?

   A Earth's orbit around the sun
   B Storm development
   C Major earthquake areas on Earth
   D Determining Earth's age from fossil records

2. On which page would you begin reading to learn about rocks and minerals?

   A 137
   B 138
   C 139
   D 142

3. In which chapter might you read about instruments used to measure temperature and wind speed?

   A Chapter Four
   B Chapter Five
   C Chapter Six
   D Chapter Seven

4. Which chapter is the shortest?

   A Chapter Four
   B Chapter Five
   C Chapter Six
   D Chapter Seven

5. On what page would you begin reading about Earth's orbit around the sun?

   A 128
   B 130
   C 132
   D 137

6. On which page would you begin reading to find out about the three main types of rocks?

   A 137
   B 142
   C 152
   D 155

7. Which information would probably be found in Chapter Seven?

   A The formation of fossils
   B Causes for the seasons
   C Weather patterns on Earth
   D Earth's history

8. On which page would you begin reading about how scientists predict the weather?

   A 170
   B 174
   C 176
   D 179

Practice 3: Study Skills

Directions: Read each question. Then choose the best answer. On your answer sheet, darken the circle for the correct answer.

1. To find the population of your state in 1950, you would look in—

   A an almanac
   B a newspaper
   C a dictionary
   D an encyclopedia

2. To find out when a play will be showing in your city or town, you would look in—

   A an atlas
   B a newspaper
   C an encyclopedia
   D a telephone book

3. To find several words that are synonyms for *angry*, you could look in—

   A a thesaurus
   B an atlas
   C a newspaper
   D an encyclopedia

4. To find information about the natural resources in your state, you could look—

   A in the newspaper
   B in an encyclopedia
   C in a dictionary
   D on a globe

5. To find the correct way to form the plural of *city*, you should look in—

   A an encyclopedia
   B a telephone book
   C a dictionary
   D a newspaper

6. You want to know if your new science book has information about the Ice Age. To find out, you might look in the book's—

   A glossary
   B credits
   C title page
   D index

7. To find the distance from Austin, Texas, to Columbus, Ohio, you would probably use a—

   A globe
   B city map
   C map of Texas
   D map of the United States

8. To find out which countries border Israel, you would probably use—

   A a magazine
   B an atlas
   C a dictionary
   D an almanac

Practice 4: Study Skills

Directions: Read each question. Then choose the best answer. On your answer sheet, darken the circle for the correct answer.

1. Which of the following sets of words are in alphabetical order?

   A whine, wholly, whart, whether
   B treat, trench, transfer, tribute
   C excess, export, extra, extreme
   D reel, reef, regiment, regret

2. The guide words on a dictionary page are *barlow–barrel*. Which of the following words would you find on that page?

   A barn
   B barren
   C barricade
   D bark

3. Which of the following could be the guide words on a dictionary page with the word *hobble*?

   A host–hostel
   B horrible–horror
   C handsome–handy
   D hive–hoggish

4. Which of the following sets of words are in alphabetical order?

   A remark, rejoice, relax, renew
   B grape, grasp, grateful, gratefully
   C shimmer, shriek, shift, shrimp
   D barn, barley, barren, bashful

5. The guide words on a dictionary page are *mobile–modern*. Which of the following words would you find on that page?

   A moan
   B mourn
   C modify
   D model

6. Which of the following could be the guide words on a dictionary page with the word *rider*?

   A ridge–right
   B riding–rim
   C rich–ridiculous
   D rhythm–rice

7. Which of the following sets of words are in alphabetical order?

   A practical, preach, prince, proper
   B goggle, golf, goblin, gone
   C review, retreat, resist, retire
   D minnow, misery, mischief, miser

8. Which of the following could be the guide words on a dictionary page with the word *sleep*?

   A slender–slim
   B sled–sleigh
   C slave–sleek
   D sleeping–slight

Practice 5: Study Skills

Directions: Read each question. Then choose the best answer. On your answer sheet, darken the circle for the correct answer.

At the library, Seema used the computer card catalog to find some books about running and jogging. Here are the title cards for two of the books Seema found. Use them to answer the questions.

Card 1

613.71

Title	On the run: exercise and fitness for busy people/by Grete Waitz with Gloria Averbuch.
Author	Waitz, Grete, 1953–
Publisher	Emmaus, PA: Rodale Press: Distributed in the book trade by St. Martin's Press, c 1997.
Description	xiv, 226 pp.: illustrated.
Notes	Includes index.
Subject(s)	Physical fitness.
	Exercise.
	Running.
	Jogging.
Other Entries	Averbuch, Gloria, 1951–

Card 2

796.426

Title	Running together: the family book of jogging: the how's and why's of jogging for fun and fitness/by Jed Cantlay, Robert Hoffman; [photographs by Al Murphy ... et al.].
Author	Cantlay, Jed
Publisher	West Point, NY: Leisure Press, c 1981
Description	112 pp.: illustrated.
Subject(s)	Jogging.
	Running.
	Physical education and training
	Family recreation.
Other Entries	Hoffman, Robert, 1947–

1. Who wrote *On the Run*?

A Jed Cantlay
B Robert Hoffman
C Grete Waitz
D Emmaus Pa

2. *Running Together: The Family Book of Jogging* was published in—

A 1912
B 1947
C 1953
D 1981

3. *On the Run* does not have—

A illustrations
B an index
C photographs
D information on fitness

4. Which of the following statements is NOT true?

A *On the Run* was published by Rodale Press.
B *Running Together* includes illustrations.
C *On the Run* has 226 pages.
D *Running Together* was published in Emmaus, Pennsylvania.

5. To find other books like *Running Together*, Seema could look under the following category of books:

A Leisure activities
B Family recreation
C Family fun
D Exercise

6. Who took the photographs included in *Running Together*?

A Al Murphy
B Robert Hoffman
C Jed Cantlay
D Gloria Averbuch

7. What is the copyright year of *On the Run*?

A 1951
B 1953
C 1981
D 1997

8. Which of the following statements is true?

A *On the Run* and *Running Together* were published in the same year.
B Both *On the Run* and *Running Together* have an index.
C Both *On the Run* and *Running Together* include photographs.
D Robert Hoffman is the co-author of *Running Together*.

Practice 6: Study Skills

Directions: Read each question. Then choose the best answer. On your answer sheet, darken the circle for the correct answer.

At the library, Clay used the computer card catalog to find some books about Thomas Jefferson. Here are the title cards for two of the books Clay found. Use them to answer the questions.

Card 1

920.02	
Title	Booknotes: life stories: notable biographers on the people who shaped America/ [compiled by] Brian Lamb
Other Title	Book notes
Publisher	New York: Times Books, c 1999
Description	xxiii, 471 pp., [32] p. of pictures; color illustrations
Notes	Collection of essays by various biographers based on interviews originally held on the television program Booknotes
Contents	George Washington, Paul Revere, John Adams, Thomas Jefferson, James Madison, Sam Houston, Susan B. Anthony, Sojourner Truth … and more
Subject(s)	Biography
Other Entries	Lamb, Brian 1941–
	Booknotes (Television program)

Card 2

Juvenile Biography–Jefferson	
Title	Thomas Jefferson/Wendie C. Old.
Author	Old, Wendie C.
Publisher	Springfield, NJ: Enslow Publishers, c 1997
Description	112 pp.: illustrated
Series Title	United States Presidents
Summary	Explores the life of the third president, from his childhood in Virginia, through his writing of the Declaration of Independence, to his years in office.
Subject(s)	Jefferson, Thomas, 1743–1826
	Presidents
Format	Juvenile

1. Who wrote *Thomas Jefferson*?

   A Brian Lamb
   B Wendie C. Old
   C Enslow Springfield
   D John Adams

2. Which of these statements is NOT true?

   A Both books include illustrations.
   B *Booknotes* includes information about several people who shaped America.
   C *Thomas Jefferson* was published in New York.
   D *Thomas Jefferson* is one in a series of books about American presidents.

3. The copyright year for *Booknotes* is—

   A 1743
   B 1941
   C 1997
   D 1999

4. *Thomas Jefferson* was published in—

   A Springfield, New Jersey
   B New York City
   C Enslow, New Jersey
   D Virginia

5. The selections in *Booknotes* are based on—

   A Thomas Jefferson's writings
   B the Declaration of Independence
   C interviews from a television program
   D magazine articles

6. *Booknotes* was published by—

   A Brian Lamb
   B Enslow Publishers
   C Times Books
   D the Booknotes television program

7. The call number for *Booknotes* is—

   A 1999
   B 920.02
   C 471.25
   D 1743–1826

8. To find other books like *Thomas Jefferson,* Clay could look under the following category of books—

   A Presidents
   B Booknotes
   C Juvenile
   D Childhood

Practice 7: Study Skills

Directions: Read each question. Then choose the best answer. On your answer sheet, darken the circle for the correct answer.

The graph shows the amount of rain that fell in Johnson City and Monroe from January through April in five different years.

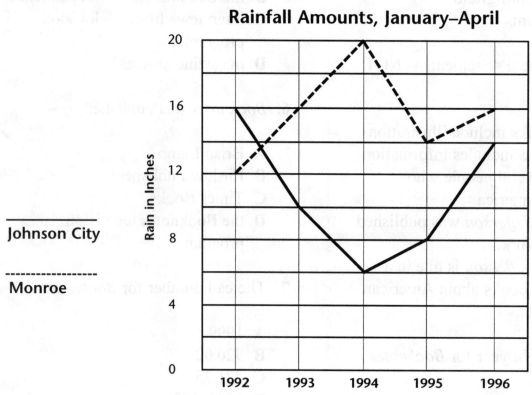

Rainfall Amounts, January–April

Johnson City

Monroe

1. In which year was there the greatest difference in the amount of rainfall in Johnson City and Monroe?

   A 1996
   B 1995
   C 1994
   D 1993

2. In 1995, how much rain fell in Johnson City from January–April?

   A 22 inches
   B 14 inches
   C 8 inches
   D 4 inches

3. In which year did it rain 2 inches more in Monroe than in Johnson City from January through April?

   A 1996
   B 1995
   C 1994
   D 1993

4. In which year did it rain more in Johnson City than in Monroe?

   A 1995
   B 1994
   C 1993
   D 1992

Practice 8: Study Skills

Directions: Read each question. Then choose the best answer. On your answer sheet, darken the circle for the correct answer.

The graph shows the number of hours the Perez children watched television during May and June of one year. Use the graph to answer the questions.

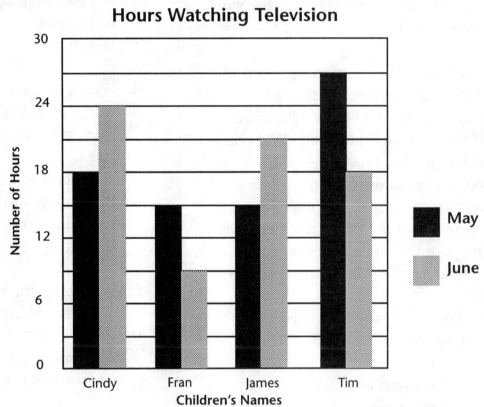

1. How many more hours of television did Cindy watch in June than in May?

   A 6
   B 12
   C 15
   D 18

2. How much less television did Tim watch in June than in May?

   A 3
   B 6
   C 9
   D 12

3. What was the total number of hours James watched television in May and June?

   A 12
   B 24
   C 30
   D 36

4. In May, how many more hours of television did Tim watch than Fran?

   A 27
   B 18
   C 12
   D 9

Practice 9: Study Skills

Directions: Read each question. Then choose the best answer. On your answer sheet, darken the circle for the correct answer.

Here is the dictionary entry for the word **groom**. Use it to answer the questions.

groom [grüm] *noun, plural* **grooms**.
1. person responsible for the care of horses: *The **groom** brushed the mare and fed her.* **2.** a bridegroom: *The **groom** was late for his wedding.* *–verb*, **groomed, grooming. 1.** to clean and condition an animal: *The man **groomed** the dog before the show.* **2.** to get ready or prepare for something: *Her family **groomed** her for a leadership position.*

1. The word **groom** can be either a noun or—

   A an adjective
   B an adverb
   C a verb
   D a pronoun

2. What does the word **groom** mean in the following sentence?

   *Mr. James hired a **groom** to work in the stable.*

   A get ready or prepare
   B clean or condition an animal
   C bridegroom
   D person responsible for the care of horses

3. What is the plural of the word **groom**?

   A groomed
   B grooming
   C grooms
   D [grüm]

4. Which of these could be the guide words on a dictionary page with the word **groom**?

   A grocery–ground
   B gross–grotto
   C grind–groan
   D gritty–groggy

5. What does the word **groom** mean in the following sentence?

   *The **groom** was nervous when he walked into the church.*

   A person responsible for the care of horses
   B bridegroom
   C clean and condition an animal
   D get ready or prepare

Practice 10: Study Skills

Directions: Read each question. Then choose the best answer. On your answer sheet, darken the circle for the correct answer.

Here is a dictionary entry for the word **reed**. Use it to answer the questions.

reed [rēd] *noun, plural* **reeds**. **1.** a tall grass that grows in wet places: *Tall reeds grow along the river.* **2.** a person who is weak or easily influenced **3.** a wind instrument in an orchestra: *The clarinet is a reed.* **4.** part of a loom used in weaving *–adjective,* **reeded**. decorated with reeds: *The chairs had reeded backs.*

1. What is the meaning of **reed** in the following sentence?

   I can depend on Joshua because he is not a reed.

   A tall grass
   B weak person
   C part of a loom
   D decorated with reeds

2. Which of these could be the guide words on a dictionary page with the word **reed**?

   A reduce–reel
   B real–red
   C reel–reflex
   D referee–refuse

3. The plural of the word **reed** is—

   A reed
   B reeded
   C reeding
   D reeds

4. The word **reed** rhymes with the word—

   A cried
   B fed
   C bid
   D lead

5. What is the meaning of **reed** in the following sentence?

   Can you hear the reeds in the orchestra?

   A decorations
   B tall grasses
   C weak people
   D wind instruments

Practice 11: Study Skills

Directions: Look at the map. It shows the region of the world known as Central America. Then read each question and choose the best answer. On your answer sheet, darken the circle for the correct answer.

Central America

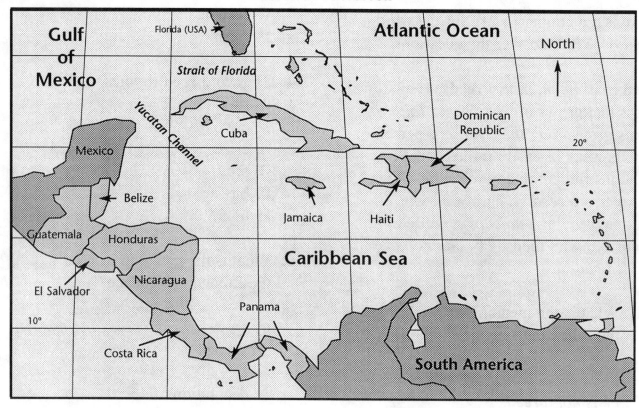

1. Which country is NOT shown as part of Central America?

   A Honduras
   B Cuba
   C El Salvador
   D Egypt

2. Cuba is—

   A east of Haiti
   B west of Jamaica
   C east of Mexico
   D south of Costa Rica

3. To travel from South America to Jamaica, you would cross—

   A the Yucatan Channel
   B Atlantic Ocean
   C Nicaragua
   D the Caribbean Sea

4. Which two countries share the same island?

   A Cuba and Jamaica
   B Dominican Republic and Haiti
   C Panama and Costa Rica
   D Belize and Guatemala

5. Which country does NOT border Guatemala?

A Belize
B El Salvador
C Nicaragua
D Honduras

6. Which country is directly north of South America?

A Dominican Republic
B Costa Rica
C Mexico
D Guatemala

7. To travel from Honduras to Panama by land, you would go through—

A Nicaragua and Costa Rica
B Nicaragua and El Salvador
C Nicaragua and Belize
D Nicaragua only

8. Which Central American country seems to be closest to Florida in the United States?

A Mexico
B Haiti
C Belize
D Jamaica

Notes

Appendix

- **Answer Key**
- **Scoring Guidelines for Open-Ended Questions**
- **Scoring Rubrics for Open-Ended Questions**
- **Vocabulary List**
- **Answer Sheet**

Notes

Answer Key: Vocabulary

Practice 1 (p. 13)
1. C 2. B 3. C 4. A 5. C
6. D 7. A 8. B 9. D 10. A

Practice 2 (p. 14)
1. D 2. C 3. A 4. C 5. B
6. D 7. B 8. C 9. A 10. D

Practice 3 (p. 15)
1. D 2. A 3. B 4. B 5. C
6. C 7. A 8. D 9. B 10. C

Practice 4 (p. 16)
1. B 2. D 3. C 4. C 5. A
6. D 7. B 8. C 9. C 10. A

Practice 5 (p. 17)
1. C 2. C 3. A 4. B 5. D
6. C 7. B 8. D 9. A 10. D

Practice 6 (p. 18)
1. D 2. B 3. C 4. C 5. A
6. B 7. D 8. C 9. A 10. C

Practice 7 (p. 19)
1. A 2. B 3. B 4. B 5. A
6. B 7. B 8. A 9. A 10. A

Practice 8 (p. 20)
1. B 2. B 3. A 4. B 5. A
6. A 7. A 8. B 9. B 10. B

Practice 9 (p. 21)
1. B 2. A 3. A 4. B 5. B
6. B 7. A 8. A 9. B 10. A

Practice 10 (p. 22)
1. B 2. C 3. C 4. A 5. D
6. D 7. B 8. C

Practice 11 (p. 23)
1. C 2. B 3. B 4. C 5. D
6. A 7. D 8. B

Practice 12 (p. 24)
1. A 2. D 3. B 4. D 5. C
6. B 7. A 8. C

Practice 13 (p. 25)
1. C 2. A 3. C 4. B 5. D
6. D

Practice 14 (p. 26)
1. B 2. D 3. C 4. C 5. B
6. A

Practice 15 (p. 27)
1. C 2. A 3. D 4. C 5. B
6. B 7. C 8. D

Practice 16 (p. 28)
1. C 2. B 3. C 4. D 5. A
6. B 7. D 8. C

Practice 17 (p. 29)
1. D 2. C 3. B 4. B 5. A
6. C 7. C 8. D

Practice 18 (p. 30)
1. B 2. D 3. C 4. C 5. A
6. C 7. B 8. D

Answer Key: Comprehension

1: A Helpful Little Lady (p. 33)
1. D 2. C 3. C 4. A 5. B
6. D 7. C 8. B 9. B 10. D
11. B 12. C 13. B 14. C 15. See
scoring guidelines and rubrics

2: A New Way to Study (p. 37)
1. C 2. A 3. C 4. B 5. D
6. B 7. C 8. A 9. C 10. B
11. B 12. C 13. B 14. & 15. See
scoring guidelines and rubrics

119

3: How the Camel Got His Hump (p. 42)
1. C 2. B 3. D 4. C 5. A
6. B 7. D 8. C 9. C 10. B
11. D 12. A 13. B 14. B
15. & 16. See scoring guidelines and rubrics

4: Giants of the Desert (p. 48)
1. D 2. B 3. D 4. D 5. B
6. B 7. C 8. A 9. B 10. C
11. C 12. D 13. A 14. See scoring guidelines and rubrics

5: A New Look at Old Maps (p. 52)
1. B 2. C 3. D 4. C 5. B
6. D 7. B 8. D 9. C 10. B
11. See scoring guidelines and rubrics

6: The Big Bear-Cats of China (p. 55)
1. D 2. C 3. C 4. A 5. D
6. B 7. C 8. C 9. A 10. B
11. D 12. C 13. A 14. C 15. See scoring guidelines and rubrics

7: The Bump (p. 59)
1. D 2. A 3. C 4. C 5. B
6. D 7. B 8. C 9. C 10. D
11. B 12. B 13. A 14. & 15. See scoring guidelines and rubrics

8: Selections by Sara Teasdale (p. 65)
1. C 2. B 3. A 4. A 5. C
6. D 7. C 8. C 9. D 10. B
11. C 12. D 13. See scoring guidelines and rubrics

9: Butterflies On the Go (p. 69)
1. D 2. C 3. C 4. A 5. B
6. C 7. D 8. C 9. B 10. D
11. A 12. C 13. See scoring guidelines and rubrics

10: Rebecca of Sunnybrook Farm (p. 73)
1. B 2. B 3. D 4. C 5. C
6. A 7. C 8. D 9. A 10. C
11. B 12. D 13. C 14. See scoring guidelines and rubrics

11: A Taste of Honey (p. 78)
1. B 2. C 3. D 4. B 5. C
6. D 7. A 8. D 9. B 10. B
11. See scoring guidelines and rubrics

12: Pandora's Box (p. 81)
1. A 2. C 3. C 4. B 5. D
6. D 7. B 8. C 9. B 10. A
11. C 12. D 13. B 14. D 15. See scoring guidelines and rubrics

13: The River Bank (p. 85)
1. C 2. C 3. B 4. D 5. B
6. D 7. A 8. B 9. C 10. C
11. D 12. B 13. B 14. See scoring guidelines and rubrics

14: How Do You Sharpen a Pencil? (p. 90)
1. D 2. D 3. B 4. C 5. D
6. A 7. A 8. C 9. B 10. D
11. C 12. C 13. C 14. See scoring guidelines and rubrics

15: Mr. Nobody (p. 95)
1. C 2. A 3. D 4. B 5. D
6. B 7. C 8. B 9. A 10. C
11. D 12. See scoring guidelines and rubrics

Answer Key: Study Skills

Practice 1 (p. 101)
1. D 2. C 3. C 4. A 5. B

Practice 2 (p. 102)
1. C 2. C 3. D 4. A 5. B
6. B 7. C 8. D

Practice 3 (p. 104)
1. A   2. B   3. A   4. B   5. C
6. D   7. D   8. B

Practice 4 (p. 105)
1. C   2. A   3. D   4. B   5. D
6. C   7. A   8. B

Practice 5 (p. 106)
1. C   2. D   3. C   4. D   5. B
6. A   7. D   8. D

Practice 6 (p. 108)
1. B   2. C   3. D   4. A   5. C
6. C   7. B   8. A

Practice 7 (p. 110)
1. C   2. C   3. A   4. D

Practice 8 (p. 111)
1. A   2. C   3. D   4. C

Practice 9 (p. 112)
1. C   2. D   3. C   4. A   5. B

Practice 10 (p. 113)
1. B   2. A   3. D   4. D   5. D

Practice 11 (p. 114)
1. D   2. C   3. D   4. B   5. C
6. A   7. A   8. A

Scoring Guidelines for Open-Ended Questions

Character Analysis

An effective response will include the following elements—

- a clear, consistent focus on the character
- specific details (e.g., the character's words, the character's actions) that support the character's description
- details that are separate and distinct

Use these scoring guidelines with the following open-ended question—

"Rebecca of Sunnybrook Farm," page 77, #14

Facts/Details

An effective response will include the following elements—

- facts that are pertinent to the main idea statement
- facts that are separate and distinct
- evidence of an understanding of the type of facts/details that logically support the given main idea
- evidence that a coherent paragraph could be written with the facts/details provided

Use these scoring guidelines with the following open-ended questions—

"A Helpful Little Lady," page 36, #15
"The Big Bear-Cats of China," page 58, #15
"Butterflies on the Go," page 72, #13

Genre Identification

When identifying the correct genre of a reading selection, students should mention several of the following characteristics—

Fiction
- use of the basic elements (character, setting, problem, solution)
- sequence of events leading to a resolution (plot)
- purpose: to entertain

Nonfiction
- emphasis on factual events/information
- purpose: to explain, argue, persuade

Poetry
- use of stanza/verse form
- focus on sounds of language (e.g., alliteration, onomatopoeia)
- use of figurative language (e.g., similes, metaphors)
- use of rhyme and rhythm

Use these scoring guidelines with the following open-ended questions—

"A New Look at Old Maps," page 54, #11
"How Do You Sharpen a Pencil?" page 94, #14
"Mr. Nobody," page 97, #12

Interpretations/Conclusions

An effective response will include the following elements—

- an introduction that clearly states the writer's opinion
- a clear, effective organizational plan
- appropriate and specific reasons that logically support the writer's position

- a clear, logical elaboration of reasons with facts, details, information, etc., from the text
- clear transitions from one part of the answer to another
- a clear, logical conclusion that summarizes the writer's position and reasons

Use these scoring guidelines with the following open-ended question—

"A New Way to Study," page 40, #14

Predictions

An effective response will include the following elements—

- an introduction that clearly states the predicted outcome
- a clear, effective organizational plan
- appropriate and specific reasons that logically support the writer's prediction
- a clear, logical elaboration of reasons with facts, details, information, etc., from the text
- a clear, logical conclusion that summarizes the writer's prediction and supporting reasons

Use these scoring guidelines with the following open-ended questions—

"The Bump," page 64, #15
"Pandora's Box," page 84, #15

Similarities/Differences

An effective response will include the following elements—

- a clear introduction that identifies the issues, characters, etc., to be compared/contrasted

- a clear, effective organizational plan to handle both similarities and/or differences
- specific details that identify similarities and/or differences
- clear transitions from one part of the response to another
- a clear, logical conclusion that summarizes the points made in the response

Use these scoring guidelines with the following open-ended questions—

"A New Way to Study," page 41, #15*
"How the Camel Got His Hump," page 46, #15
"Giants of the Desert," page 51, #14
"Selections by Sara Teasdale," page 68, #13
"The River Bank," page 89, #14*

*These questions do not require a written composition as a response. To evaluate them, focus on the student's selection and use of specific details that identify similarities and differences.

Summarize Ideas/Themes

An effective response will include the following elements—

- a clear focus on the text's major ideas
- omission of extraneous details/information
- a clear, accurate statement of the text's basic message/content

Use these scoring guidelines with the following open-ended questions—

"How the Camel Got His Hump," page 47, #16
"The Bump," page 63, #14
"A Taste of Honey," page 80, #11

123

Scoring Rubrics for Open-Ended Questions

In most states that administer tests with open-ended questions requiring student-written responses, evaluators use scoring rubrics to assess these responses. A scoring rubric is an assessment tool designed to determine the degree to which a writer meets the established criteria for a given writing task.

Many scoring rubrics allow for holistic evaluation, which focuses on the overall effectiveness of the written response rather than individual errors in content, organization, mechanics, etc. For example, a scoring rubric might allow a teacher to score papers on a scale from 1 (for the least effective responses) to 4 (for the most effective responses). Rubrics that offer a broader scale of points (e.g., 1–6) allow for a more refined evaluation of a written response. For example, with these rubrics it is possible for evaluators to distinguish between an outstanding response (e.g., 6) and a very good response (e.g., 5). Rubrics with a narrow scale of points (e.g., 0–2) do not allow for a very refined evaluation, generally limiting evaluators to a response of either "pass" or "fail."

Sample scoring rubrics appear on the following pages. They offer several options for evaluating the written responses students complete for the open-ended questions in *TestSMART®*. A brief description of each rubric follows.

Note: Teachers may also use scoring rubrics provided for their own state's competency test.

Three-point rubric: This rubric has a narrow scale of points and, therefore, limits the scoring to basically pass–fail. The two-point rubric is most appropriate for brief written responses (2–4 sentences). In addition, this rubric works well with the short answers recorded on graphic organizers (e.g., Venn diagrams).

Four-point rubric: This rubric provides a wider scale of points, making a more refined evaluation possible. It does not, however, allow teachers to make clear distinctions between outstanding responses and those that are merely good. The four-point rubric is appropriate for brief written responses (2–4 sentences) and longer responses (two or more paragraphs).

Six-point rubric: Because of the broad scale of points, this rubric allows for a more refined evaluation of a written response. The six-point rubric is appropriate for longer responses (two or more paragraphs).

Three-Point Rubric

2 Provides complete, appropriate response
Shows a thorough understanding
Exhibits logical reasoning/conclusions
Presents an accurate and complete response

1 Provides a partly inappropriate response
Includes flawed reasoning/incorrect conclusions
Overlooks part of question/task
Presents an incomplete response
Shows incomplete understanding

0 Indicates no understanding of reading selection
Fails to respond to question/task

Four-Point Rubric

4 Focus on topic throughout response
Thorough, complete ideas/information
Clear organization throughout
Logical reasoning/conclusions
Thorough understanding of reading task
Accurate, complete response

3 Focus on topic throughout most of response
Many relevant ideas/pieces of information
Clear organization throughout most of response
Minor problems in logical reasoning/conclusions
General understanding of reading task
Generally accurate and complete response

2 Minimal focus on topic/task
Minimally relevant ideas/information
Obvious gaps in organization
Obvious problems in logical reasoning/conclusions
Minimal understanding of reading task
Inaccuracies/incomplete response

1 Little or no focus on topic/task
Irrelevant ideas/information
No coherent organization
Major problems in logical reasoning/conclusions
Little or no understanding of reading task
Generally inaccurate/incomplete response

Six-Point Rubric

6
Full focus on topic throughout response
Thorough, complete ideas/information
Clear, maintained organizational pattern throughout
Clearly logical reasoning/conclusions
Thorough understanding of reading task
Accurate, complete response

5
Focus on topic throughout most of response
Very thorough ideas/information
Clear organization throughout majority of response
Generally logical reasoning/conclusions
Overall understanding of reading task
Generally accurate and complete response

4
Focus on topic/task but with obvious minor digressions
Sufficient relevant ideas/information
Minor gaps in organization in parts of response
Minor problems in logical reasoning/conclusions
Above average understanding of reading task
Minor inaccuracies that affect quality and thoroughness of response

3
Focus on topic/task but with obvious major digressions
Relevant ideas/information mixed with irrelevant material
Major gaps in organization
Somewhat logical reasoning/conclusions
Basic understanding of reading task
Several inaccuracies that affect quality and thoroughness of response

2
Little or no focus on topic/task throughout response
Few relevant ideas/pieces of information included in response
Lack of organizational plan
Illogical reasoning/conclusions throughout response
Lack of basic understanding of reading task
Generally inaccurate/incomplete response

1
Unacceptable response due to severe problems in focus, relevancy, organization, and/or logical reasoning/conclusions
No understanding of reading task

Vocabulary List

absent
abundance
admiral
admitted
affect
afterward
agriculture
allergic
amber
ambition
amuse
angel
ankle
arch
arouse
assume
astonish
atmosphere
award
ballad
barley
barren
bashful
bawl
behavior
bison
blank
blister
boulder
bribe
brocade
bruise
budget
cabinet
café
calculate
candidate
celebration
chemical
chowder
circuit
circular
civilization
clasp
cleat
clog
clot
coarse
college
colonial
commit
committee
commotion
compact

composition
conceive
concentrate
conference
confess
confuse
constellation
consume
continent
contrary
conversation
corridor
courage
creak
crest
delay
demand
development
device
diet
disgust
dispose
distress
earnest
elbow
elder
electronic
emblem
emergency
enclose
encourage
envy
equipment
errand
especially
eve
expedition
export
extraordinary
extreme
fabric
fertile
fertilizer
fiction
flicker
foreign
fortunate
fraction
framework
frantic
frontier
fulfill
funeral
fungus

furnish
fuse
garment
gasp
generation
geography
geology
glee
gleefully
glimpse
glisten
globe
goblin
goggles
golf
grasp
grateful
graze
gymnasium
haul
heap
hedge
hemp
hermit
hoarse
holy
hood
horrify
hull
hymn
imitate
immortal
impression
incident
indicate
indignant
influence
inherit
injure
inner
innocent
innumerable
inspect
instance
invader
investigate
jagged
jealous
jealousy
jersey
jewelry
junior
lame
lee

license
lieutenant
limestone
loan
loft
logo
loyal
magnificent
mammoth
mansion
marvelous
mature
minnow
mischief
misery
mistress
mortal
murmur
musket
mutton
napkin
nephew
nevertheless
nonfiction
notion
offend
opal
operate
ornament
orphan
pagoda
parakeet
parlor
patriot
pavilion
peculiar
peddler
penetrate
phonograph
phrase
pier
plank
plantation
poll
portion
practical
preach
precaution
precise
principle
proceed
production
profession
professional

profit
progress
pronounce
protest
purse
rage
ragged
rascal
ravine
reality
reception
reef
reel
reflect
refuge
regiment
regret
rejoice
relax
remark
renew
republic
reputation
research
resent
resist
resource
restore
retire
retreat
review
revolve
rigid
rumor
sacred
sacrifice
sapling
savage
scar
scorpion
scroll
scuff
seldom
select
sergeant
series
shift
shriek
shrink
simmer
sincere
sire
slaughter
slick

slight
slump
sly
snatch
snorkel
sober
sorrow
spar
spit
splotch
spurt
squire
stain
stallion
steed
strife
stunned
submit
superintendent
superior
surf
surrender
survey
swarm
tackle
telegram
temporary
tempt
temptation
terrace
theme
theory
thicket
thrash
throb
topic
torment
tragedy
traitor
tramp
transfer
transparent
tread
treason
treat
treaty
trench
trial
tribute
triumph
trudge
twinkle
unite
universe

university
urge
utter
vague
valuable
various
vary
vault
vein
venison
veterinarian
visible
volunteer
wade
wail
ward
warehouse
warrant
weary
wharf
whine
wholly
width
worship

Name _____   Date _____

Vocabulary: Practice # _____   Study Skills: Practice # _____

Comprehension: Passage # _____

Answer Sheet

1. (A) (B) (C) (D)   8. (A) (B) (C) (D)

2. (A) (B) (C) (D)   9. (A) (B) (C) (D)

3. (A) (B) (C) (D)   10. (A) (B) (C) (D)

4. (A) (B) (C) (D)   11. (A) (B) (C) (D)

5. (A) (B) (C) (D)   12. (A) (B) (C) (D)

6. (A) (B) (C) (D)   13. (A) (B) (C) (D)

7. (A) (B) (C) (D)   14. (A) (B) (C) (D)